The Wittgenstein House

Bernhard Leitner
The Wittgenstein House

Princeton Architectural Press

Published by
Princeton Architectural Press
37 East 7th Street
New York, NY 10003
www.papress.com
1-800-722-6657

© 2000 Bernhard Leitner
All rights reserved
04 03 02 01 00 5 4 3 2 1 First English edition
Published simultaneously in German edition
by Hatje Cantz Verlag

ISBN 1-56898-251-8

Printed in Germany

No part of this book may be reproduced
in any manner without permission of the publisher
except in the context of reviews.

Design and Layout
Bernhard Leitner

Computer Assisted Graphics
Beatrix Bakondy

Production
Gabriele Sabolewski

Typesetting and Reproductions
Weyhing digital, Ostfildern-Ruit

Translation
Camilla R. Nielsen and James Roderick O'Donovan

Project Editor, US-edition
Mark Lamster

Special thanks to Nicola Bednarek, and the staff
of the Princeton Architectural Press

Library of Congress Cataloging-in-Publication Data
is available from the publisher.

Front cover
Dining room; photo by Bernhard Leitner/Elisabeth Kohlweiß.

Back cover
Ludwig Wittgenstein's pocket photo album;
photo by Moritz Nähr, reprinted with permission from
the Wittgenstein Archive, Cambridge, England.

Preface	9
Notes	10
Kundmanngasse	22
History	36
Saving the Wittgenstein House (1969–1971)	39
The Pocket Photo Album	49
The Urban Context	59
Hall, Double Doors	64
Salon	82
Sitting Room/Bedroom	90
Dining Room	96
Beak-shaped Catch	102
Lighting	114
Metal Curtains	119
The Colors of the House	128
Floor/Joint Plan	138
Pillar Hall	152
Staircase	160
Radiators	168
Handles	170
Door Hinges	180
Reading Wittgenstein	188

Preface

The Wittgenstein House refers to my book *The Architecture of Ludwig Wittgenstein* that was published in 1973. The interconnection of the two books, which span a period of almost three decades, is underscored by a similar format, the size of some reproductions (160 x 160 mm), and the reprinting of some photographs , including illustrations of architectural elements and details that were an integral part of Wittgenstein's building but no longer exist today. In 1976, New York University Press published a reprint of the documentation in identical form. In 1995, it was republished in London without my approval—not as a reprint but with a completely distorted layout of images and texts.

From the perspective of the 1973 book, the building appeared very static. Through this emphasis on the static, dignified aesthetics there is a danger to assume that Wittgenstein's early philosophy has been translated into architecture and that his logical thought could explain this seemingly austere architecture. In 1971, Thomas Stonborough sold the house to a Viennese developer who subsequently had all the trees sawed down or poisened.[1] To avert the danger of vandalism the same owner had all of the terrace doors of the building welded in 1972. This factor added to the rather hermetic character of the house in my 1973 documentation.

The house *appears* to be static. Motion is an intricate part of Wittgensteinian architectural aesthetics. How doors and window-doors are opened and closed, the way one interacts with the house, the way spaces interweave, how light reflects on the polished lacquered, color surfaces of the floor, metal doors and walls—all of these factors give the building its temporal dimension. Many aspects of Wittgenstein's aesthetics can only be deciphered through time and movement. The present publication, *The Wittgenstein House*, is an attempt toward a sharper observation of the house.

---

[1] While I was working on the book, Heinrich Postl wrote me a letter on September 30, 1972 in which he reported the following. "In 1971, all of the trees, save for eight that surrounded the house, were sawed down, six were killed off by pouring a chemical substance into a hole that had been drilled into the tree. Only two trees were spared. In 1972, they were all sawed down." Heinrich Postl had been a pupil of Wittgenstein's from the time he taught in Puchberg. Since Margarethe Stonborough had "asked [me] in the most amicable way whether I would like to work for her" he worked as a housekeeper, taking up this job when the house was still under construction. Postl worked in the house until 1971.

Notes

1

Architecture cannot be applied philosophy. Only a clichéd misunderstanding can refer to this multi-layered, complex art of architecture as "logic translated into a house" (Hermine Wittgenstein). Wittgenstein's architecture is intended to be and indeed must be read and understood in the language of architecture. It should not be treated as philosophy translated into a building or as applied thought.

2

Through the process of building and his intense preoccupation with architecture, Wittgenstein learned something about himself, he experienced an artistic revelation. This led him to questions that had a bearing on his philosophical work.

3

Ludwig Wittgenstein never explains his architecture. Only his questions and descriptions illustrate how he built and how he found a very specific form that has validity to him and cannot be exchanged with anything else.

4

In 1973, Cyrill Barrett quoted in a letter various excerpts from Wittgenstein's lectures on aesthetics from the summer of 1938, adding: "… they gave a picture of Wittgenstein busy designing and building that house … and they have all the more force for *not being directly reminiscent*."

5

If it were not for the building, it would be difficult to imagine an architecture by Ludwig Wittgenstein. Verticality does not figure in his writings. His language games are forms of thought that bear no relation to pictorial forms.

6

Wittgenstein's aesthetics have various roots: his will for clarity, simplicity, exactness, and his fine-tuned sense for consistent, millimeter-precise proportions, and a unique understanding of mechanics and its laws. Wittgenstein's architecture is not a depiction of mechanics, as widely seen in the art of the 1920s (Léger, Eisenstein, Chareau).

7

Wittgenstein's aesthetics is rooted, to a substantial degree, in the laws of mechanics.

8

The house in motion refers to the house in use. Use is not functionality (the path between sink and stove). Use is action such as opening a door, interlocking window-doors or raising metal curtains. Ludwig Wittgenstein gives movement form based on the laws of mechanics. In contrast to the machine aesthetics of the twenties, movement to Wittgenstein is mechanics: lever, weight, support, energy, friction.

9

There is a technical, scientific aspect in Wittgensteinian aesthetics, directly deduced from Newtonian laws as opposed to the "pseudo-technoid" vocabulary of classical modernism (machine aesthetics).

10

One of the most puzzling aspects of Wittgenstein's architectural work is his aesthetics of weightlessness. He selected metal as a material to achieve acumen and precision. Yet, owing to his detailed knowledge of mechanics, the laws of energy, the translation of force and friction, he succeeded in dissolving the weight of metal. The weightless movement of heavy metal doors and metal curtains cannot be depicted. It only becomes visible in use or once in motion.

11

While Mies van der Rohe lowers vast glass surfaces (as in the Tugendhat House) by means of switches and electric motors (an abstract/non-sensual triggering of movement), Wittgenstein transforms the play of force between weight and weightless movement of the metal curtains into a gesture of sensual experience.

12

In Ludwig Wittgenstein's architecture mechanics is not to be read as a sign of industrial production or as a metaphor for the new, industrially manufactured product. The beauty of his tall metal doors lies in their precision, their dematerialized, shiny surface. They derive their beauty even more from movement and gesture. How little physical effort is required to move weight.

13

Wittgenstein did not approach design from an economic point of view. (This runs counter to modern architecture, which considers economics a significant parameter of design). In the Wittgenstein House everything is by special design. Metal is not an expression of new construction technology nor does it symbolize progress (Le Corbusier). Metal (and its inherent characteristics) and mechanics inspire Wittgenstein in his thinking and lead him to new ideas. Mies van der Rohe builds expensively, since he works with expensive, valuable materials (onyx, for example). Wittgenstein, however, spares no production costs when translating his architectural ideas into material form.

14

In Wittgenstein's architecture simplicity does not mean functionality-objectivity. Austerity is not an expression of modesty. Reduction is minimal, multi-layered form.

15

There is no relation to Mies van der Rohe's reduction and simplicity. The formal autonomy, the immanent beauty and natural history of an onyx block, which Mies van der Rohe used as a central design element in the Tugendhat House, is "inconceivable" for Wittgenstein. All of the materials used by Wittgenstein are "artificial" or "unnatural." The conceptual framework of his architecture is complete control over all elements and how they interrelate. This excludes the use of marble or exotic wood. Despite his purely artificial material idiom, Wittgenstein succeeds in lending his architecture a high degree of sensuality and warmth.

16

Wittgenstein's nervous system is the "natural" element of his building—deviations that are necessary for him (for example, free raster networks versus geometric raster rigidity: joint plan of the artificial stone slabs on the floor.)

17

There is a Wittgensteinian beauty in the house that cannot be deciphered via ratio, logic, or mechanics. The eye does not find rest in a building that rests within itself.

18

What appears to be self-contained, hermetic or austere in Wittgenstein's architecture opens up when touched by the eye or the hand.

19

Positions of doors, axial views, inconspicuous details—the eye continually discovers things that are surprisingly consistent. The reductive formal idiom is easier to read with the knowledge of later developments in art (such as abstraction and minimal art).

20

Transitions are significant not only in music for the gestalt of a work. Transitions as metaphors of movement. Full metal doors = closed surface. Translucent glass door = allusions of spatial depth. Transparent glass door = view into the room.

21

In the process of working with architecture, by his unique way of posing questions, Wittgenstein finds radically new solutions that are unprecedented in twentieth-century architecture.

22

For Wittgenstein, no form stylistically results from another one; the door handle has nothing formally in common with the recessed capital. They are both, along with everything else, the result of a very specific will to form, a very special form-finding process, a very unique way of thinking. This attitude ultimately binds all of the parts and forms together. One cannot really speak of a stylistic repertoire with regard to Ludwig Wittgenstein. In a different hall he might not have designed the capital and the beam to form a double recess.

23

Any additional work is fully justified for Wittgenstein, as long as it enables him to realize his idea and to find the most reduced and most meaningful form.

24

Wittgenstein's architecture cannot be deduced from his writings. His intention is manifest in the building. The process leading to art is not reversible.

25

One cannot find any interpretation of the house in Wittgenstein's writings. One should not look for them there.

26

Wittgenstein creates a self-contained architecture from which no academic ideas can be deduced, nor a single form extracted. The marketing of a so-called Wittgenstein handle is a perversion of the Wittgensteinian form-finding process.

27

Wittgenstein's construction transcends Loos and his notion of architecture.

28

It is indicative of the quality of the building that Wittgenstein created harmonious, static spaces and details, but did not combine them together as a set of separate building blocks. In lieu of a mechanical, modular order everything here refers to everything else, relates to each other, is connected to each other geometrically as well as conceptually.

29

Modern architecture wants to express its revolutionary social thrust—the liberation of man and the open plan cannot be separated from each other. There is little connecting Wittgenstein to modern architecture. Glass, transparency, metal. Yet he demands a processing of metal, a millimeter precision in construction, that was almost impossible to attain with the means of his period. This was criticized by L. Rentschler: "The apriori concept with its lacking empirical backing has its structural analogy in the demand for precision alien to any tradition of artisanship."[1] A reproach based on a misunderstanding of art: Wittgenstein's will to form is the measure. He literally forces the material into his conceptual construction. It is only in this way that something truly exceptional could emerge.

[1] In: Gebauer, Gunter et al. *Wien. Kundmanngasse 19*. Munich 1982.

30

Mies van der Rohe designs the consummate artistic beauty of a new, open space where man and nature become united in a higher, cosmic entity. For this space Mies van der Rohe considers in his very first sketches the positioning of the furniture he has designed for the space. Wittgenstein, by contrast, creates a self-referential architecture, independent of the zeitgeist:

each piece of furniture, be it modern or historical, will have its effect on this architecture and will come to bear—if it has aesthetic quality. This, too, distinguishes Wittgenstein's building from the avant-garde of his time.

31

Wittgenstein analyzes a movement and gives it shape.

32

Wittgenstein does not allow any curtains or carpets. He does not want them to cover his architecture like a second skin. Their inherent imprecision counters the precise spatial boundaries and transitions.

33

Calling Wittgenstein a dilettante is based, like so many other misunderstandings, on the preconceived view of the onlooker. He sees what he wants to see or can see, he does not let himself be drawn into Wittgenstein's art of building. He finds faults where there are none. When he does not understand a solution, he speaks of lacking ability to design, whereas Wittgenstein deliberately deviates from the usual solution. He seeks to prove conceptual errors related specifically to the discipline whereas Wittgenstein apparently develops a different professional approach.

34

You cannot measure the building with inaccurate or inappropriate measuring instruments.

35

Puzzling shifts in proportions are not necessarily conceptual fallacies of an architect lacking expertise.

36

Wittgenstein seeks harmony, timelessness, and tranquility. He thus strives time and again for form and symmetry—down to the last detail. He accomplishes this in an intricate, asymmetric structure. Yet, in his architecture there is neither the dynamic spatial idea of modernity nor the smooth modular, formalist classicism with its alignment of axes. Wittgenstein applied in a compelling way an approach based on diametrically opposed poles, closed versus open, static rooms versus an asymmetric, joint-like, shifted spatial structure.

*And when I hold the ruler against the table,
do I always measure the table,
might I not sometimes be checking the ruler?*

Wittgenstein's handwriting
(Original size)

Manuscript: *Philosophische Bemerkungen XVII*
Trinity College, Cambridge

37

Wittgenstein had at least one tool that he could use for building, namely his knowledge of mechanics and the laws of mechanics, his mastery of the constructive processing of metal. Yet, no single metal element in his architecture appears to be the technical, verifiable result of a mechanical engineering draftsman. (Wittgenstein had studied several semesters of mechanical engineering at the Technical University Charlottenburg in Berlin.) For him, thoughts and feelings are the prerequisite for precision, not the graph paper. For working with sculpture, by contrast, he had no artistic tool which is apparent in his only piece of sculpture, the head of a girl. This sculpture does not clarify anything, it does not invent anything.

38

Ludwig Wittgenstein had a deep understanding of music but he did not listen to the music of his time. Evidently, he did not need it, it did not interest him, nor could he develop any real interest in modern architecture.

39

To say something old with new means. (How would this manifest itself in music?) In his architecture he succeeds in doing this—expressing something radically new using the vocabulary of tradition.

40

Wittgenstein's architecture leads to the stringent logic of emotion.

41

The glass doors create opening and transparency. The additional (though not technically necessary) vertical mullion reduces the transparency of the doors. Given the height of the doors its narrow form is difficult to manufacture. The vertical subdivisions of the door and window wings figure most dominantly in Wittgenstein's aesthetics. They heighten the sense of verticality and stringency.

42

The most significant thing about the building is its proportions—certainly the most mysterious determinants of architectural quality. The parts and the whole complement each other in their proportions. The ratio of proportions and dimensions relates to each other and then again it does not. It is intuition that determines the proportions.

43

Wittgenstein could sense the most subtle nuances in the rendering of a musical idea (from Bach to Bruckner). In this way, and only in this way, can something be said... But he is not at all interested in the development of new and innovative musical concepts.

44

Wittgenstein has no language, no vocabulary for building. His idiom of design—regarding space, materials, colors, and details—had to be invented and discovered through the work. This finding and inventing is part of every artistic process.

45

A person and his/her signature. From this an attitude can be deduced, a way of thinking, evaluating, questioning, deciding. Attitude and mode of thinking are part of the aesthetic result. They do not, however, decipher it.

46

As opposed to reading or thinking, looking is physical, an all-encompassing process. Scanning the height (body size) and the distance (step/movement), walking and seeing, movement and measuring. Reading with the body—in architecture, in front of a picture, within sound.

47

Field of vision. Wittgenstein repeatedly poses questions related to "seeing." What do I see, how? Imprecision in seeing, as opposed to precision of the form. How do I see a surface in the light? A color next to another one? How do I feel this material, this diversity of materials? How do I move through the geometry of a building? He reflects on the boundaries of vision and color.

48

In his writings Ludwig Wittgenstein jots down a number of ideas in two, even three ways. He does not want to decide on one specific word form, i.e., he wants to let a concept, an idea oscillate in different directions. Multiple forms of expression are more open-ended and thus more precise. In the art of building space is *one* decision, *one* possibility.

49

What is precision in architecture? Defining a modular system? Or that which appears consistent to our senses?

50

Wittgenstein's building *appears* to reflect the highest precision, conveying an impression of exactitude, stringency and clarity. Wittgenstein also underscores this by his recourse to symmetry from which he again and again deviates. He notes: "meaningful irregularity."

51

Numbers/symbols

Ludwig Wittgenstein's preoccupation with sequences and series of numbers. His distinction between "physical and visual number."

If one refers to the "only" opening on the main floor (the glass doors which are merely vertically divided) by the number 1, various numerical images result.

1 + 1 + 1 + 1   Dining room inside (all leaves closed)

1 + 1 + 1 + (1)   Dining room inside (with door open to the hall)

1 + 1 + 1   Dining room (view of southwest terrace)

(1) + 1 + 1   Wall of salon (with opened metal wings)

1 + 1 and 1 + 1   Northeast terrace (view of salon and sitting room/bedroom)

52

Paul Engelmann plays a special role as a go-between. As poet, philosopher and architect he links the various intellectual threads of Viennese modernism. He is one of those rare, important artists who make one aware of connections and live them. He mediated between various artistic areas, between persons.

53

Force without violence. On the contrary: stuccolustro, yellow shimmering surface like a taut, lush skin.

54

It is strange how exactitude can also be ambivalent. Dematerialization of material is achieved through varnished or polished color surfaces.

55

Wittgenstein shows the highest simplicity, gives the impression of modesty, a "modesty" that is barely affordable.

56

Park and building. A strange sensuality—Wittgenstein did not "allow" any flowers in the garden, only green, variations of green.

57

Referring to his thinking Wittgenstein said: "I think I have never *invented* an idea. Rather it was always given to me by someone else, and I have then with great passion immediately incorporated it into my endeavor to clarify thought. In this way, Boltzmann, Hertz, Schopenhauer, Frege, Russell, Kraus, Loos, Weininger, Sprengler, Straffa influenced me."

58

Wittgenstein's architecture cannot be a direct depiction of his philosophical thought. Wittgenstein's building can be deciphered on the basis of Wittgenstein the person. It is the same thinker. It is the same thinker who is trying to solve architectural issues here. His building is simultaneously an expression of his exceptional artistic-sensual talent and his potential to translate an idea into form. Proof of this is the building itself.

59

One has the impression that one looks at fundamental architecture, yet at the same time one is aware of its extreme artificiality.

60

Wittgenstein has a fine sense of proportion. His architectural thinking reveals unusual self-assurance in the process of finding form, in material and formal design. Only this way does the building become an intellectual-sensual phenomenon.

61

In spite of the symmetry and axes, in spite of the rigid geometry and the number games (4:2, 4:1, 3:1, 2:1), the proportions, in addition to the materials, make the building stand out. They are perhaps the best indication of architectural quality.

62
The impression Wittgenstein's architecture makes is significantly defined by the fact that he reduces doors and window-doors to one element—a glass door consisting of four narrow, vertical surfaces or a double glass door. They are all by special design and individually manufactured, differing only by a few centimeters in the width of the glass surfaces or in the distance between the double glass doors. However, they appear to be one and the same element, which makes the architecture even more emphatic. Here one finds neither the conventions of door and room nor that of wall and window. The repetition of one element triggers an unconscious counting. The emphatic nature of a litany-like structure in which the addition of an element is both form and content. In spite of this repetition of elements, the house itself is one single visual gesture (cf. Brancusi's *Endless Column* in Tirgu Jiu.)

Kundmanngasse[1]

Vienna III, Parkgasse 18 (summer 1927)

My dear Keynes,... (I have) taken up architecture. I am in the process of building a house in Vienna. This is causing me considerable worry and I am not even certain that I won't botch it. As ever, yours, Ludwig

Vienna III, Kundmanngasse 19 (1928)

Dear Keynes, I have just finished my house, which has occupied me entirely over the past two years.... I enclose a few photos and hope that you don't find its simplicity too offensive. As ever, yours, Ludwig

At the time of completion Wittgenstein wrote a letter to the company which had carried out the metal works:

Construction Palais Stonborough, Vienna, November 10, 1928

To M. Weber & Co. in Vienna

Since your work on my building is now nearing completion, I am obliged and also feel the need to express my thanks and appreciation to you for your outstanding achievements. I can honestly say that without your work it would have been impossible to create this building with the precision and expertise necessary for a design of this kind. I am convinced that no other company in Vienna would have been in the position to fulfill what I had to demand in a similar manner.... I express my highest esteem and remain sincerely yours,

L. Wittgenstein

"My house." "My building." "What I had to demand...." Two years of intensive work by Ludwig Wittgenstein on an architecture, on architecture.

---

[1] The "Palais Stonborough," as Ludwig Wittgenstein termed his building in a letter dated November 10, 1928 to the Weber company, lies between Kundmanngasse and Parkgasse in Vienna's third district. The site office was located in a single-story building on the Parkgasse side. Vehicular and pedestrian access was from Kundmanngasse no. 19. Within the family and among friends the house was known as "Kundmanngasse."

On November 27, 1925 Paul Engelmann, a student of Loos, wrote in a letter to Ludwig Wittgenstein, a friend of his since 1916, that Wittgenstein's sister Margarethe Stonborough wanted to build a mansion in Vienna. She had doubts whether this would be possible "nowadays" and Engelmann thought "rather no than yes but [I] would, if I received the commission, dare to make an attempt. I would very much like to talk to you about these and other, more important, matters." Before Engelmann accepted the commission, he wanted to talk to Wittgenstein about "these matters." At the beginning of December, Wittgenstein answered: "I look forward to seeing you in Vienna at Christmas. Building a house would also interest me greatly." Did Wittgenstein and Engelmann talk about building a house at the end of December 1925? Together or separately, with the client Margarethe Stonborough? Did Wittgenstein merely listen? That was not his manner.

Engelmann described the collaboration between himself, Margarethe Stonborough, and Ludwig Wittgenstein during the first planning phase in a letter he wrote from Tel Aviv on February 16, 1953 to Professor F. A. Hayek in Chicago:

"L. W., who worked as a teacher at that time, took a great interest in this project and whenever he was in Vienna offered excellent advice, so that I finally had the feeling that he understood Mrs. Stonborough's intentions better than I. She herself took an active part in working out the design. Her participation revealed the greatest degree of taste and a high level of culture and yet the result of this collaboration was not entirely satisfactory for either party. For this reason, and as Wittgenstein found himself in a severe mental crisis after having given up his job as a teacher, I suggested to him that he should carry out the building together with me. After having thought over the matter for quite some time, he accepted my idea. This solution turned out to be a fortunate one for both him and the building. From that point on, he was actually the architect and not myself. Although when he started working on the project the plans had already been completed, I view the result as his and not as my own achievement."

Whose ideas do the floor plans reflect? Were they "completed" and is it true that they were not further altered, as Paul Engelmann remembered twenty-five years later?

In chapter V of her *Familienerinnerungen* (Family Recollections, written in April/May 1945), Hermine Wittgenstein noted: "Engelmann drew up the plans for the house together with Gretl and with her constant collaboration. Then Ludwig came along and took an interest in the plans and models in his own intense manner; he began to alter them and became more and more involved in the matter until he finally took it over. Engelmann had to give in to a far stronger personality and the house was built, down to the smallest detail, according to plans altered by Ludwig and under his direct supervision."

In February 1926, a copy of the entry in the land register referring to a site that was under consideration for her building was prepared for Margarethe Stonborough by a civil engineering office. The site lay behind her parents' palais in Vienna IV, Argentinierstraße 16 (previously called Alleegasse). As Otto Kapfinger first pointed out in 1989, her house was originally planned for a courtyard situation with problematic access in an urban block. It was only in late spring that the planning concept was transferred, without major re-planning, to the newly acquired plot in Vienna III, Kundmanngasse 19, a building site open on three sides to the surrounding streets.

The highly self-assured client decided on Paul Engelmann as the architect although he had not planned or completed any major designs by himself. There is no indication that she had considered any other architects although there were numerous highly acclaimed architects in Vienna at the time—such as Loos, Frank, Strnad, Hoffmann, or the young Plischke, as well as experienced architects from the rigorous Wagner school. She chose Paul Engelmann partly because she knew him as a friend of Ludwig's who had carried out smaller alterations for her family but primarily because she wanted to participate in the design and to incorporate her lifestyle and culture in the building. Her program of spaces can be clearly read in the very first sketches: representative rooms for entertaining, music, dining, library and, characteristically, a terrace in front of those spaces with tall window-doors. She knew what she wanted. The idea was that Engelmann should transfer her "intentions" which, according to his own statement, he could not completely understand, to the plans and the building itself. Thus, from the very start Engelmann's sketches developed with the continuous involvement and under the influence of the client. Therefore, his sketchbook should not be interpreted as a documentation of the way in which Engelmann's ideas for the building evolved.

At Christmas 1926, Paul Engelmann made Margarethe Stonborough a present of the sketchbook. In this book he collected design ideas dating from April and May 1926. This sketchbook gives the impression that Engelmann did not translate the commission into an architectural language of his own. This fact is particularly apparent in the first sketches.

It has always been maintained that Paul Engelmann first involved Wittgenstein in the design process in autumn 1926 or summer 1926 and that the plan was developed by Paul Engelmann. The circumstantial evidence contradicts this assertion.

In the period from December 1925 until the end of April 1926, Wittgenstein had, as Engelmann reported, offered "excellent advice." This advice certainly did not aim at improving a Loosian approach but was rather advice that "better" complied with his sister's "intentions," more so than Engelmann's ideas. The issue cannot have been about stylistic details but principally about the sense of space and the layout. Margarethe did not want a house characterized by Loos' ideas of "comfort" and without doubt Wittgenstein introduced ideas which expressed his own way of questioning and thinking. It seems inconceivable that he was not familiar with the plan drawn to a scale of 1:100 by Paul Engelmann and dated May 18, 1926 which clearly illustrates Margarethe Stonborough's ideas. Given Margarethe's close and trusting relationship with her brother, with whom she discussed everything, we must assume that Wittgenstein was involved from the very start in the planning and that he contributed his own architectural ideas.

In accordance with Wittgenstein's own wishes, his letter of resignation as a teacher is dated April 28, 1926. In a letter from April 19, 1926 to his friend Koder, he writes: "In a week I will start to work as a gardener's assistant." At the end of April, Wittgenstein, who had resigned from teaching, wanted to start working for the Brothers of St. John of God (Hospitallers) in Vienna Hütteldorf. It has always been maintained that he worked as an assistant gardener for several weeks in Hütteldorf. In the archives of the religious order there is a staff record book in which the names of all kitchen staff, cleaning staff, casual laborers, tailors, garden workers etc. between 1913 and 1950 are precisely recorded. Even those who worked for only a few days are registered. For the months between April and November there is not a single indication that Wittgenstein worked there. His name simply does not appear. There is not even an indication that he worked for a trial period. Consequently, from May 1926 onwards Wittgenstein was constantly in Vienna again. He most likely started work in the site office in May or perhaps at the beginning of June. Engelmann writes that he had asked Wittgenstein, after he had given up working as a teacher to "carry out the building together with me." The "excellent advice" which led Engelmann to make this suggestion refers to the time up to the end of April.

Although compelling proof can never be offered for the development of creative ideas, it seems likely that the motif of a central hall with reception rooms arranged around it, which suddenly appeared in Engelmann's sketchbook, was put on paper by the architect after having received "excellent advice" from Wittgenstein, following discussions between the brother and sister and the architect. The motif of a central hall from which one gains access to the representative rooms has its roots in the tradition of Viennese palais architecture. In the planning of Margarethe Stonborough's mansion the hall represents more than an intention to link the Palais Stonborough to this Viennese tradition. Margarethe was just as familiar with this type of building as her brother Ludwig: it refers to the central hall with a single-flight staircase in their parents' palais in Alleegasse (Kapfinger 1989). Wittgenstein's approach was to adopt ideas and forms as stimuli and to then "purify" and "clarify" them. In his parents' palais the single-flight staircase led towards a wall, at the center of which a sculpture by Drobil, a friend of the family, stood on a column-like base. In the sketch plan which Engelmann put on paper on May 18, 1926 the single-flight staircase (in this case rising only half a story) leads towards a wall at the center of which a square base for a plaster cast of the Discus Thrower is drawn. Even at this early planning stage Wittgenstein and his sister wanted to incorporate the sculpture. Following completion of the house at the end of 1928, the sculpture was indeed integrated at this very position. Various perspective sketches by Engelmann note this idea which can only have come from Margarethe and Ludwig. The hall lends the building its "family resemblance."

The sketch plan from May 18, 1926 has a main architectural idea that speaks a clear language: a central hall with adjoining music, dining and breakfast rooms. This part complies with the "intentions" of the client and her aspirations. This part is also worked out thoroughly and the axes, rhythm and connections are all clearly drawn. Obviously, this is where Margarethe and Ludwig made their contribution. The other rooms in the sketch plan reveal a very different spirit. They may well have been designed from outside as elements in the composition of the building block but as interiors they are not fully thought out, nor are they drawn with the same conviction. Stairs, niches, walls of shelving and a passageway flanked by columns have the scale of intimate rooms in a "comfortable" bourgeois apartment. They are related to the spirit of Loos' school of building which did not comply with the client's "intentions."

The sketch plan (May 18, 1926) is not a completed floor plan. Nor, as is often asserted, was it merely minor alterations to this sketch which led to the final plan. Wittgenstein created the

Sketch plan of the main floor, drawn by Paul Engelmann on May 18, 1926.

In this plan Paul Engelmann combined the client's ideas
with the "excellent advice" (Engelmann),
Wittgenstein contributed from the very beginning of the planning process,
and his own concepts that were strongly influenced by Loos' architectural thought.

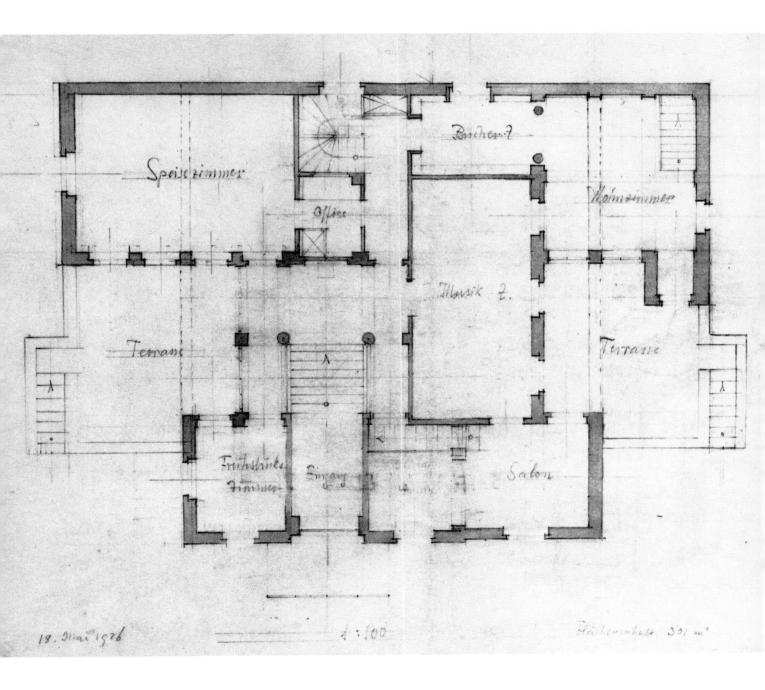

final floor plan as illustrated in the working drawings dated November 15, 1926 to form a densely woven mesh of spaces achieved by making significant alterations to the proportions, by expanding the layout and by making two decisive additions (spatial sequence entrance—vestibule—hall and staircase). This architecture is, despite its asymmetry, a kind of "absolute, complete" formation that is solidly and complexly put together and in which nothing can be changed and indeed nothing was changed. It is completely in Wittgenstein's spirit and by his hand.

In the 1:50 plan dating from November 15, 1926 the concept of the central configuration of spaces is adopted. The proportions of the dining and breakfast rooms are almost unaltered. Small but decisive increases in size turn the former music room into the salon. The hall, which in the sketch was still completely square, now becomes a space that can be read on a number of levels within Wittgenstein's overall design. It has a particular orientation both with regard to its dimensions (6.50 x 6.85 m) and the design of the ceiling and yet, as a result of the arrangement of the pilasters, it is apparently without a dominant direction. The hall forms a calm center but at the same time it is the termination of Wittgenstein's newly conceived solution for the entrance: a room extended somewhat in the direction of the entry, followed by a completely square second vestibule and then by the hall, which is separated by a glass wall. These are arranged to form an almost ritualistic sequence of spaces that clearly reveal the character of the house. The proportions of this sequence of spaces are modest in comparison to the impression made by the architecture. Representation with no trace of pomposity—something which cannot be said of the late nineteenth-century hall in the palais Wittgenstein on Alleegasse.

Everything in the sketch plan from May 18, 1926 which was reminiscent of Loos' ideas on dwelling was eliminated. These rooms were redesigned by Wittgenstein in the spirit of the central space and "interlocked" within his overall composition: the living room on the southwest with the library and the sitting room/bedroom for the client. Margarethe Stonborough, like Thomas Jefferson, placed her bed in an opening accessible from both sides in the eighty-centimeter-wide wall element between her living area and her wardrobe/dressing room. On the northwest side a bathroom, a servant's room and a pantry attached to the dining room were added: Wittgenstein probably reached his decisions, in particular with regard to sleeping area and service rooms, in accordance with his sister's wishes. Engelmann was involved but in his own words was "not actually the architect."

Working drawing as finalized by Wittgenstein dating from November 15, 1926.

This (somewhat edited) plan demonstrates how Wittgenstein condensed the spatial layout: he altered the proportions, created a new intimate living area for the lady of the house (sitting room/bedroom), redesigned both terraces and their connection to the garden, inserted a twelve-pier hall housing the main staircase and elevator and transformed the entrance into a "ritual" sequence of spaces.

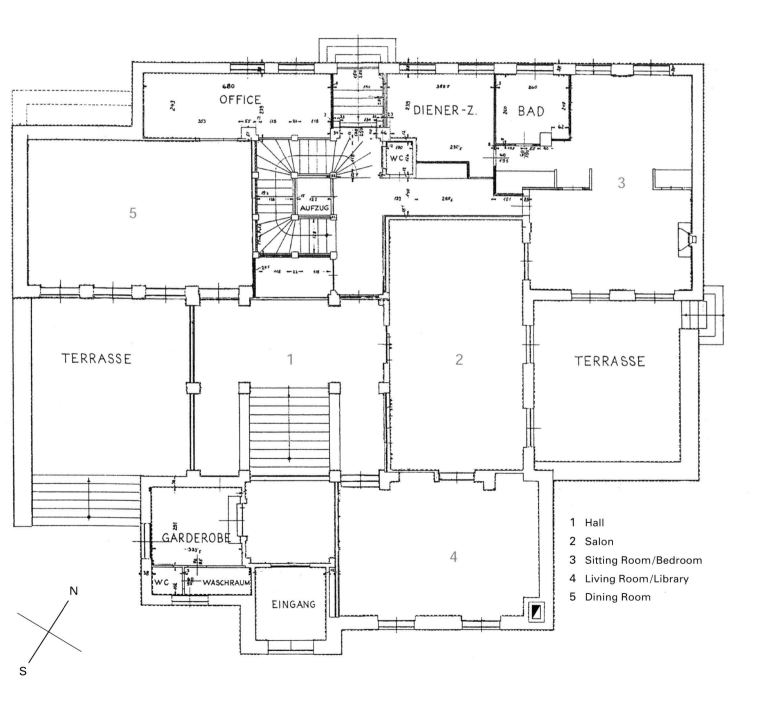

1 Hall
2 Salon
3 Sitting Room/Bedroom
4 Living Room/Library
5 Dining Room

With the staircase and elevator Wittgenstein introduced a significant building idea. It is a twelve pier structural system inserted into the building where technology is clearly displayed. A radical aesthetic decision for a domestic building.

After the war Wittgenstein wrote in a letter that the house had been built for the family. He therefore regarded it as desirable that his eldest sister, Hermine, who had remained in Austria, should move into the house, after it had been used for a different purpose during and after the war. The youngest sister, Margarethe, was still living in emigration in the USA. On January 24, 1946 Wittgenstein turned to the third sister, Helene (Salzer), in Vienna from Cambridge: "Mining [Hermine] wrote to me that it is not out of the question that she might some day live in Kundmanngasse. There is nothing I could wish for more, no matter what she hangs on the walls and even if she puts curtains in front of the windows. Anything is better than that this house, which cost so much, should stand senselessly there. After all, it was built for the family and although it is suited to Gretl and, in a certain sense, unsuited to the two of you, this lack of resemblance remains at least within the *family*."

In 1928, he had forbidden Margarethe to furnish the rooms with curtains, carpets and chandeliers. He would be understanding should the other sister wish to employ such furnishings as long as the house was used again by the family and remained within the family. This architecture was neither obliged to nor indeed wished to accept social responsibility (in the narrow ideological and political sense of the term) for that which did not expose itself to public critique (in the narrow sense of the Zeitgeist), was for Wittgenstein a building for the family.

This house, created with the greatest degree of intellectual acumen and at considerable financial expense, is the result of a rare constellation. In Margarethe Stonborough Wittgenstein had found a client who was as self-assured as she was understanding and who appears to have been completely convinced of her brother's various abilities. At first, the intention was that the untrained architect would work with Engelmann. When Wittgenstein wanted to undertake the entire responsibility for the building and ultimately did, she supported whatever her unusual genius brother demanded and designed. (There is no evidence that she sought to organize any compromises with Engelmann). On the other hand, Wittgenstein ascribed the building only to this one member of his family: the house is "suited" only to Margarethe. Margarethe Stonborough viewed and used the architecture quite naturally as

Working drawing dated November 15, 1926 superimposed on the sketch plan dated May 18, 1926.

Wittgenstein thinks the sketch plan through, alters and condenses it, making it ultimately into a floor plan that is entirely his own.

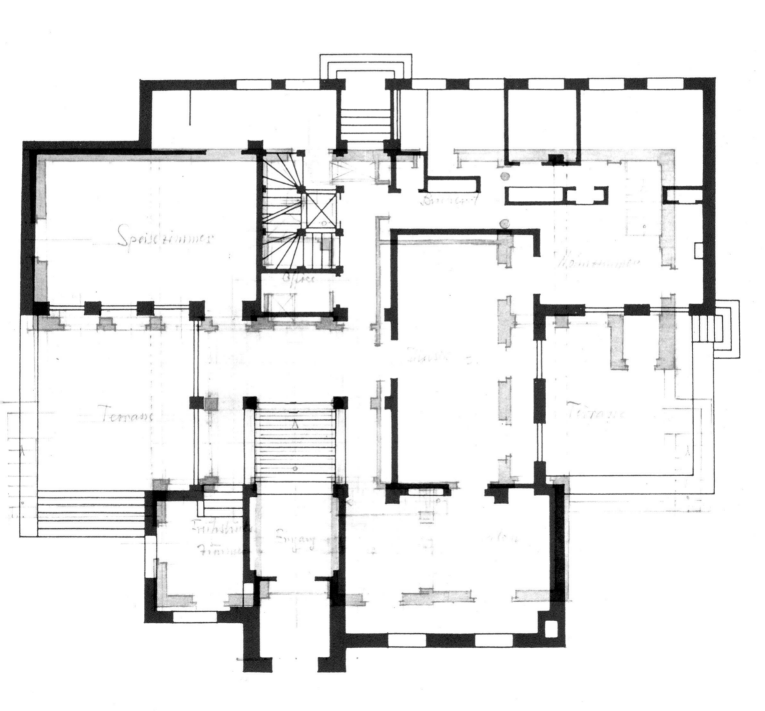

her house. She found it perfectly natural that this architecture was not "comfortable" and was purely a private matter.

Adolf Loos on the other hand writes: "The work of art is a private matter of the artist. The house is not. The work of art is given to the world without any given need. The house responds to a need. The work of art is responsible to no-one, the house to everyone. The work of art aspires to shake people out of their comfortable ways. The house must serve to provide comfort." (Adolf Loos. *Trotzdem*. Innsbruck 1931.)

Margarethe, herself an extremely well educated and strong willed woman with an interest in the arts, knew the sensitive, critical culture of her brother Ludwig. She could not know that he possessed an enormous talent for architecture. This manifested itself in the course of dealing with the challenge, in the process of working on the building. Wittgenstein had no experience how an art work could be given a valid form and statement. He had no experience how an architectural work must be completed. Therefore, in the course of building he felt some insecurity, and feared that he might "botch" the project. In the middle of construction, Wittgenstein could not foresee whether he would succeed in translating his architectural thought into his own material language. Only the final result would show if he succeeded artistically and whether the work so intricately conceived was "right."

His architectural thinking has nothing to do with traditional ways of working with materials. His solutions, apparently simple, could be carried out only with great effort and by taking neither time nor money into account. His sister was willing to have executed whatever his aesthetic form intent demanded as the only "right" solution. "… I admire my sister Gretl who let him have a free hand in this matter. Two great people came together as architect and client, enabling something complete within itself to be created in this building. Equal attention was paid to the most insignificant detail as to the main issues because everything was important. Nothing was unimportant, except time and money." (Hermine Wittgenstein, *Family Recollections*.)

After completion the building did not receive a single mention in the professional field of architecture, nor was it documented in any specialist periodical, let alone discussed. In the period after 1928, Moritz Nähr made a number of photographs of the new building for the family. Wittgenstein, who self-confidently added the term "architect" to his signature, was not interested in making his achievement known in a field whose ideological and aesthetic discussion he did not wish to take part in. Distrustful as he was towards progress in the area of architecture and music, he was never in a position to participate in such a discussion.

"Not as if I didn't know," Wittgenstein writes in the preface to a planned publication of the manuscript *Philosophische Bemerkungen* (Philosophical Remarks), which was to be published in 1930, "that what today claims to be architecture is not architecture . . . ." and he continues "it is not as if he (the author) did not view what is termed modern music (without understanding its language) with the greatest distrust . . . ." Wittgenstein clearly distances himself from modernism: "It is clear to me that the disappearance of a culture does not mean the disappearance of human values but merely of certain means of expressing these values, yet the fact remains that I view the direction of European civilization without sympathy and without understanding for its goals, if indeed it has any. Therefore, I write in fact for friends scattered throughout the four corners of the world." (WA3.111.1)

At the end of the 1920s, Adolf Loos had his office on Beatrixgasse not far from the Kundmanngasse building site in the same district of Vienna. The building contractor, Friedl, who also worked for Loos, was Wittgenstein's builder. Jacques Groag was also involved at the same time in both the construction of Adolf Loos' Moller house on Starkfriedgasse and on the building on Kundmanngasse. However, not a single letter or note or indication exists that Loos, who had known Wittgenstein for years, ever visited the site or viewed the completed building. If such a visit did take place, and the various personal interconnections would suggest that this was the case, then no comment on Wittgenstein's architecture has been handed down, nor does any comment from other Viennese contemporaries exist.

Can it be that, at the apogee of classic modernism, it was not possible to see and understand the radically new quality of this architecture, which did not owe anything to the spirit of modernism? Even the Loos student, Paul Engelmann, originally entrusted with the commission and who, in fact, wanted to produce a work of his own, i.e. something related to Loos, could not, as he later admitted, "see" what kind of architecture Wittgenstein was creating.

In a conversation which the author had with Ernst Plischke, the leading architect of the International Style in Austria, on June 27, 1988 Plischke said: "We knew that he was building a house. Not interesting. After all he used factory windows. Wittgenstein was a dilettante. We did not even bother going there."

This expensive architecture was immune to criticism because its justification lay within the family. It neither sought nor received any public resonance. Margarethe Stonborough's son and heir had his own reasons to view the building as a family matter. In contrast to his mother who desired, inspired and animated the unusual qualities of this house (through the "family resemblance"), for him the important issue was to be able to decide alone about its fate, that is, about selling the property. As a result, the unknown and above all unacclaimed house slipped into obscurity until the late 1960s.

The clear distance the building keeps to both the avant-garde and to progress, which was intended from the very start, yet was in no way programmatic, gave it its particular aura. The aura of a puzzling "foundling" built at the zenith of modernism. One aspect of this aura of peculiarity and puzzlement is the question, repeatedly posed, as to how a philosopher could manage such a difficult and complex building project. The answer is to be found in the building itself.

Hardly anyone wanted or was able to read the radical quality of this architecture which cannot be ascribed to any vocabulary of modernism. As a consequence, Wittgenstein's architectural achievement never received recognition.

"The question, assuming that the building was planned or for the most part designed with the collaboration of Ludwig Wittgenstein, is whether we are dealing here with architecture or a talented dilettantism, whether it is a 'document' or a curiosity such as, to use a comparison, a piece of wood carving by Sigmund Freud would be. And Wittgenstein? He was no architect, never occupied himself with architecture. It was so easy at that time to usurp this title … he concocted the hypocaustic heating, the polished concrete floor, the bunker doors and, as light fittings, naked light bulbs hung by a cable from the ceiling …." (Dr. Peter Pötschner, Office of Landmarks Preservation Vienna, quoted in *Die Presse* April 10, 1970.)

As late as 1978, the Czech architectural historian, Vladimír Slapeta, wrote: "Wittgenstein's part was apparently initially confined to smaller alterations or additions to the layout but at a later stage, more significantly, he was involved in the detailing of the carpentry work and the doors and window handles as well as the furnishings …."[1] This superficial perception overlooks the fact that in this architecture that relationship between building and furniture which is typical for the period from the Secession up to Mies van der Rohe simply does not exist. A fundamental part of Wittgenstein's architectural thought is that he does not think in terms of modernist ideas of living. He built architecture, not a domestic or stylistic form. His building stands outside the manifestations of the avant-garde as illustrated in the single-family houses by architects from Frank Lloyd Wright to Pierre Chareau in which everything, down to the furnishings, is designed by the same architect. The furniture was provided solely and entirely by Margarethe Stonborough. The superficial view overlooks the fact that there is no "carpentry work" in the central architectural formation on the main floor where the essence of Ludwig Wittgenstein's architecture is made manifest. Wittgenstein used no "natural" materials such as wood. He worked and designed using only artificial materials whose tolerances he himself could determine down to the millimeter.

Wittgenstein built a different kind of privacy. This is not a question of taste but rather one of attitude. This attitude becomes evident in the sense of space of the individual rooms, in the tightly woven spatial connections, in material, color and details. In Wittgenstein's architecture one cannot be separated from the other. Everything determines everything else. Even when Wittgenstein takes the "traditional form" as his starting point (as, for example, he does in the case of the hall and the handrail), as a result of his radical way of clarifying things, he makes it completely new, something entirely his own. Everything becomes part of his intellectual method, as well as a part of a profoundly complex built form. As in his philosophical writings, one can start to read at any point and one is always led to or arrives at the essence of his thinking and of his way of giving form.

[1] Vladimír Slapeta: "Paul Engelmann und Jacques Groag, die Olmützer Schüler von Adolf Loos." In Ursula A. Schneider, ed. *Paul Engelmann. Architektur, Judentum, Wiener Moderne*. Vienna 1999, p.103.

History

On October 20, 1926, the City Council of Vienna gave Mrs. Margarethe Stonborough-Wittgenstein the necessary permission to build a free-standing family residence. The client had acquired the 33,000 square-foot site of a former horticultural nursery in the spring of 1926. New zoning regulations had made parts of the site available for residential use.

In November 1928, the Stonborough family moved from the Palais Schönborn, Vienna I, Renngasse 4, into the new house in Vienna III, Kundmanngasse 19.

In 1939, Margarethe Stonborough spent her last Christmas in Vienna. In early 1940, she left Vienna and spent the war years in New York. Some of the furniture that had been removed to a store house in 1940 was destroyed during the war. From 1940 to 1945 the house was used by the Red Cross as an army hospital. In 1945, Russian soldiers (and their horses) moved into the building, and later it was used as a demobilization center.

Margarethe Stonborough returned to Vienna in 1947. She lived in the house until her death in 1958 at the age of 76. Her son, Dr. Thomas Stonborough, inherited the building.

In May 1965, the southwestern half of the site was rezoned, permitting housing construction up to a height of fourteen meters. In June 1971, the northeastern part of the site was rezoned for commercial use. Now a tall skyscraper could replace the Wittgenstein House.

At this point, Thomas Stonborough sold the house to the Viennese real estate developer Franz Katlein. As a result of the massive protest actions beginning on June 21, 1971 (see pp. 39–47), the Wittgenstein House was declared a landmark on July 26, 1971. This decision was challenged in court by Katlein.

As early as February 1972, an alternative project was presented under the auspices of the Austrian Architectural League and the Central Union of Architects. Instead of the high-rise towering over the Wittgenstein House a lower horizontal building block with reduced F. A. R. was proposed to retain some air space and garden. Katlein flatly rejected the proposal, insisting on taking full economic advantage of the site. There were no further interventions. The house remained vacant and dilapidated. The Austrian government was not interested in purchasing the building designed by Ludwig Wittgenstein.

In May 1975, Katlein sold the southwestern garden section to the main federation of Austrian Social Security institutions. A fourteen-story high-rise was erected as planned, completely disregarding the very existence of the Wittgenstein House.

In December 1975, Katlein sold the Wittgenstein House to the People's Republic of Bulgaria. The selling price for lot and house was six million Austrian shillings. In the purchase contract Katlein's construction company was commissioned to adapt the building for use as a cultural institute, including the construction of a new auditorium.

Bulgaria deserves credit for saving the Wittgenstein House from further dilapidation in 1975, caused by the scandalous disinterest of Viennese political cultural authorities. In the subsequent renovation, the outer appearance of the building remained unchanged (only the northeast terrace was altered.) On the second floor three smaller rooms were merged to create a conference room, and a library was built next to the staircase. Alterations were also made in the basement and in the space leading to the new auditorium.

Severely distorted was the central configuration on the main floor. To this day it is claimed that this mutation is justified by the new use of the building: lectures, exhibitions and concerts require larger rooms. These did not exist in Wittgenstein's original building. Thus, two essential walls were torn down. One in Margarethe Stonborough's sitting/bedroom and one between salon and living room/library. This demolition changes character and meaning of Wittgenstein's architecture to such extent that it cannot be justified by any new use claim.

The original lighting, i.e., naked light bulbs suspended from the ceiling, which actually from 1928 onward had to be supported by free standing lamps, was replaced by central lighting tracks with spots. Unfortunately, all of the door handles that were later cast do not correspond to the form of the original handle. All of the matt metal pieces and metal doors were coated with a dull layer of paint in 1976 which does not come anywhere close to the original shade—this happened with the approval of the Office of Landmarks Preservation.

Since 1977 the adapted and renovated building has served as the cultural institute of the Bulgarian Embassy.

Saving the Wittgenstein House from Demolition—June 1969 to June 21, 1971

A Documentation

1 THE INCEPTION

In October 1968, I moved from Vienna to New York. In spring 1969, I met Annette Michelson, an art critic, professor of cinema studies at New York University and contributing editor of the then leading art journal *Artforum*. In June 1969, we discussed Viennese modernism and its dual talents: Schönberg and Kokoschka. In this context, I mentioned the building that Ludwig Wittgenstein had constructed in the twenties. There was great interest for Wittgenstein in the New York art scene. Annette Michelson, who was both amazed and curious, asked me to write an article with photographs on the Wittgenstein House for *Artforum*. This marked the beginning of my efforts to save the Wittgenstein House. What no one in New York or Vienna knew: Dr. Thomas Stonborough, the son of Wittgenstein's sister Margarethe, heir and owner of the house, had already at that time decided that he "had" to sell the house.

Both experts and the public knew nothing about the inside of the house. The owner regarded his house as his private business over which he wanted to deal with as he wished. He did not want to give strangers access to the house and he did not want the house declared a national monument.

At my instigation, Stonborough allowed me to tour the house and to publish in New York, but not in Vienna, an article with photographs of the interior of the house. It was from New York that all efforts originated over the next two decisive years to save the Wittgenstein House from demolition.

2 THE VISIT

On July 15, 1969 I met Stonborough at the house on Kundmanngasse 19. With his permission I took five or six photographs in his presence: not enough to attract attention to the architectural quality of the building. From today's perspective it is hardly conceivable that the building was literally unknown. Heinrich Postl, a servant employed in the house since 1928, mentioned to me on leaving that I could come again the next day in the afternoon to take more photographs. At this time Mr. Stonborough would be absent. Thus, the first photographic documentation of the Wittgenstein House materialized within a few hours on July 16, 1969.

During this visit on July 15, the "collaboration" with Stonborough to save the building began. An ambivalent, unconscious collaboration that was ultimately unintended. In conversations and, most significantly, in the six letters he wrote me between December 1969 and July 1970, he openly informed me of his intentions. Without these letters, the Wittgenstein House would no longer exist.

Stonborough wanted to sell the house; it was too large for him to manage. Moreover, he was not really fond of it. He allowed me to promote interest in the house in the United States, perhaps so as to find an institution that would be interested in buying the building. In the fall of 1969, I repeatedly talked about the house with Ada Louise Huxtable, architectural critic of the *New York Times*. But how could one sell something that no one knows?

3 THE ARTICLE

As agreed, in November of 1969 I sent my *Artforum* text to Stonborough so that he could check it. I had learned the historical facts from my talks with him. He was in complete agreement with my architectural analysis of the building.

Letter 1 (December 2, 1969): "Thank you very much for your letter of November 17 and the copy of the article you wrote about the house. I find it excellent…. It is good to hear that there is quite a lot of interest shown in New York for my uncle's house." The final sentence, however, was extremely disturbing: "I personally would prefer if we could sell the house to an institution that would maintain the building instead of having to sell it here, in which case it would certainly be demolished."

My article, "Wittgenstein's Architecture," appeared in *Artforum* (pp. 59–61) in February 1970 with fourteen selected photographs—from the hallway to the door handle—and exact descriptions. Thus, the international public was informed for the first time about the unique architectural significance of the interior spaces of the main floor.

Before the article appeared, I received letter 2 (January 22, 1970): "At the bottom of my heart I am rather pessimistic that your attempt to save the building will be able to help the patient in time, but you never know. The application for rezoning of the building site has already been submitted." The process was already under way.

Pleased about my article and my efforts, he wrote me letter 3 (February 16, 1970): "I cannot even tell you what it would mean to me if you could find a buyer for this building. I will have to sell it, but I would forever have a bitter aftertaste if the building was sold to someone who would not maintain the building and have it torn down. Almost like a bird which soils its nest."

These efforts were intensified:

January 21, 1970: First interview with Dr. Gleissner, Austrian Consul General in New York.

February 13, 1970: Letter to Dr. Gleissner, describing the most recent development. The lack of interest and understanding displayed by other official representatives of Austria in New York was disheartening.

On February 22, 1970 the *New York Times* published a long commentary referring to my *Artforum* article. In the article titled "Rescue," an appeal was made to save the building: "…now there is a one-man movement afoot to save the single house. The movement is Bernhard Leitner, a young Austrian architect, over here on a stint with the city's Office of Midtown Planning and Development…. Declaring that 'immediate acquisition is the only way to preserve this unique monument,' Leitner suggests that it could be used by a university or an international center. 'The prestige of the philosopher and architect Ludwig Wittgenstein will reflect on any future owner,' he holds …."

Artforum, March 1970: "I would like to add an urgent postscript to my article 'Wittgenstein's Architecture,' because there is a very real and present threat that the building will be destroyed …." This update had not been agreed upon with Stonborough.

4 THE SUBTITLE

Dr. Rudolf Walter Leonhardt, head of the feature section of the weekly paper *Die Zeit* in Hamburg, wanted to reprint "Wittgenstein's Architecture." Since I was obliged by Stonborough not to comment on the recent developments, I passed the necessary information on to Leonhardt in a letter dated February 4, 1970 (e.g., "The costs for Ludwig Wittgenstein's building are demolition costs.") Using this information, he wrote a brief introduction.

On February 20, 1970 my article appeared in *Die Zeit* as "Der Philosoph als Architekt" (The Philosopher as Architect). The subtitle ran: "The only house Ludwig Wittgenstein designed is in danger of being demolished." Subtitle and editorial preface about a possible sale of the building were completely in accord with my strategy. Diverse responses followed.

4.1 In his letter of February 27, 1971 Max Bill expressed his interest in the building and its fate. If he could somehow be of help to me, I was to turn to him. (In June 1971, I was thus able to propose Max Bill as one of the three experts to evaluate the aesthetic qualities of the building which would justify declaring it a landmark.)

4.2 Stonborough (in his letter of February 27, 1970) denounced "the journalistic 'sales techniques'" and wrote: "Sensationalism, that is both the subtitle suggesting the demolition and the paragraph referring to the sale of the building, are counter to my intentions. They were quite damaging to me…. I plead with you to refrain from making any statements in the United States or in Europe either on the possibility of local negotiations on a potential sale or on the demolition of the building. Under no circumstances!" In other terms: The fate of this architecture lies entirely in the hands of the heir.

4.3 The imminent threat became for the first time evident in Vienna where the legal decision-making process was already under way. Newspapers such as *Arbeiter Zeitung* and *Die Presse* published short reports on the article in *Die Zeit*.

5 THE LETTER TO THE EDITOR

On March 10, 1970 a letter to the editor appeared as an answer in *Die Presse*: "With regard to the Wittgenstein House, the author could have seen with his own eyes that the building is in good condition and the house entirely inhabited. As the owner maintains, Bernhard Leitner's statements about an intented sale or even demolition have no grounds. The gloomy prediction is nothing but sensationalism. It remains to be seen whether this is conducive to the cause of landmarks preservation. Dr. Peter Pötschner, Office of Landmarks Preservation, Vienna I."

6 THE OFFICE OF LANDMARKS PRESERVATION

The Office of Landmarks Preservation, which had been obviously misinformed, wanted to stifle the debate. Moreover, Dr. Pötschner, who was responsible for the case, attacked the Wittgenstein House in unambiguous terms: "Such a strange structure is open to any interpretation. Spleen and cupiditas rerum novarum can lead to tintillating effects but they alone cannot create true form. And any architect could be degraded to a mere accomplice if one were to substract the 1000 wishes and ideas of the client from the overall artistic achievement…." (Typed script of an article by Dr. Pötschner for *Die Presse* of April 10, 1970.) The Office of Landmarks Preservation officially and obstinately not only questioned the artistic merits of the house but also Wittgenstein's central role in designing it. Possibly after having spoken with the owner, who, after all, was eager to sell. This made it even more difficult to save the house.

I now contacted a number of philosophers and students of Wittgenstein. They wrote to the Austrian Consulate General in New York to protest the impending demolition and attest that the building was actually by Wittgenstein. "This is the only significant artwork that I know of that was created by an outstanding philosopher." (Max Black) In mid-May 1970, the letters from Prof. Max Black, Prof. Norman Malcolm, Prof. Stewart Brown and Prof. von Wright were forwarded "to appropriate authorities" in Vienna.

In August 1970, Dr. Thalhammer, president of the Landmarks Preservation Commission, mailed his reply to the Consulate General: "It is obvious that in the long run the single-family house designed for a grand bourgeois style of life cannot be maintained as a residence. There is no real reason to declare it a landmark since the artistic value of the house as well as Wittgenstein's role as architect are dubious … ."

At that time Stonborough, the owner, and the Office of Landmarks Preservation were claiming that Paul Engelmann had built the house. However, from my conversations and correspondence with Stonborough, I knew that Wittgenstein was the actual architect. A phone call to Professor von Wright, one of Wittgenstein's students, confirmed this. When he met with Paul Engelmann in Tel Aviv, Engelmann confirmed that the house was built by Ludwig Wittgenstein. This most significant statement was again confirmed many years later in the letters Paul Engelmann had written to Hermine Wittgenstein and to Friedrich Hayek.

7 A SUSPICIOUS SILENCE

Further attempts were made to find a suitable buyer abroad.

April 6, 1970: Letter to Phyllis Lambert.

In June 1970, the architect Sandy Wilson and the journal *A. D.* in London were interested in printing my article with the photographs. An additional note was to direct attention to the sale of the building, while also exerting international pressure. (The material appeared in the issue of June 1971, at that time deliberately without any commentary.)

July 6, 1970: Visit with Max Bill in Zurich.

July 13, 1970: Letter to Max Bill. "Your idea to buy the Wittgenstein House for representative purposes and as a residence for the Swiss ambassador seems to be the best and most sensible one given the circumstances … ."

In Letter 6 (July 15, 1970), Stonborough wrote: "It was especially kind of you to organize such a long meeting with Bill. In principle, the idea is great and there's nothing I'd prefer more than to sell the whole building to the Swiss government. But I wonder whether Mr. Bill is also certain that the Swiss are looking to buy an embassy … ."

Officially, there was no noticeable progress in the matter.

The initial stir in Vienna after the publication of the *Zeit*-article was apparently short-lived. But the relative calm was deceptive, since a permit for zoning change had already been applied for in January (see Letter 2).

8 NEW YORK—VIENNA—NEW YORK

Realistically, it was an illusion that any initiative could succeed against the powerful political, urban planning and economic interests in Vienna. Nevertheless, I was committed. It proved to be advantageous that colleagues from my days as a student in Vienna were now working in official positions that made it possible to monitor the developments. Therefore, I was very well informed through phone calls and letters about how the case was proceeding.

March 1971: Message that a group (lawyer, developer and realtor with intimate ties to Vienna's City Hall) has an option on the house. The plan: a skyscraper hotel on the very site of Wittgenstein House.

June 3, 1971: The City Planning Commission of Vienna approves the development and rezoning plan. There was no public or private response to the announcement in the newspapers.

9 THE INTERVENTION

June 11, 1971: Arriving from New York, I planned to spend several weeks in Vienna.
I was well informed about the state of the affairs. I knew that on June 18, 1971 the Vienna City Council was to approve the application for rezoning which would set the groundwork for demolition. In this precarious situation there was only one option left: to convince politically influential decision-makers that Wittgenstein had actually designed the building.

June 16, 1971: Meeting with the Head of the Planning Commission. His answer: too late. The Office of Landmarks Preservation had given a negative response.

My detailed letter of June 17, 1971 to the Federal Chancellor Kreisky or his secretary did not have any impact. I was told there was neither interest nor time for me to personally present the case.

The very last resort was the Ministry of Science and Culture which was also responsible for Landmarks Preservation. I presented to Mrs. Hertha Firnberg who was the minister, the six letters that Stonborough had written to me. In these letters the truth about who built the house was documented. Mrs. Firnberg did not have to comprehend the revolutionary artistic quality of the building but she had to recognize what the Office of Landmarks Preservation was unwilling to acknowledge: Wittgenstein was the architect of this building. Cultural and historical considerations alone made it imperative to declare the building a landmark. The following day, the six letters were returned to me. As a result of my intervention, Mrs. Firnberg tried to have the vote on the zoning change postponed and ordered a reexamination of the landmark status.

10 REZONING

Arbeiter-Zeitung, June 19, 1971: "The unanimity in the deliberations on the construction of a hotel on Kundmanngasse [were] disrupted by a Mr. Leitner, an architect, demanding that the house built by Wittgenstein on the site should be declared a landmark. The City of Vienna has only taken up the issue to the extent that the City Council is to approve the rezoning plan for the site, which took place yesterday (with ninety-three against seven votes)... The Ministry of Science and Culture that was asked to intervene against the resolution of the Vienna City Council declared that after extensive investigation of the Wittgenstein House by the Office of Landmarks Preservation no grounds were found for protecting the building. Moreover, there are doubts as to whether the building was actually designed by Wittgenstein. Nonetheless, the Minister of Science and Culture, Dr. Hertha Firnberg, has agreed to reexamine the issue..."

Die Presse, Vienna, June 19 and 20, 1971: "At its meeting on Friday the City Council voted for the demolition of the Wittgenstein House, Liberals and DFP voted against. During the discussion the philosopher's name was never mentioned. After the intervention of the architect Bernhard Leitner, Federal Minister Firnberg tried on Friday morning to have the rezoning removed from the agenda. For formal reasons the City of Vienna, however, rejected this demand. Independently of this, the landmark issue is to be discussed once again, since Minister Firnberg ordered the Office of Landmarks Preservation to reevaluate the building. Since Mr. Pötschner adhered adamantly to his position that the building was not designed by Wittgenstein and denied that it was worth protecting, there is not much to be expected from a resumption of talks with him."

11 EPILOGUE

On the day the site was to be rezoned, I confronted the general public with the matter once again in a long, sharply worded article. After all my past experiences it no longer made any sense to base my argument on the pure aesthetic quality of the house. In *Die Presse* of June 18, 1971 I presented all factual evidence to expose the lies surrounding the question of Wittgenstein's achievement.

12 THE CALL

If the Office of Landmarks Preservation had not reacted to this epilogue, the Wittgenstein House would have been demolished in 1971. Even though I had vehemently questioned the expertise of Dr. Pötschner, I received a call from his office the very same day. It was Friday afternoon. I was asked to come to the Wittgenstein House on Monday, June 21, 1971. Once and for all, Pötschner wanted to end the criticism directed at his far-reaching decision—in front of a small group which had been hastily called together.

13 THE RALLY

I had to turn the situation around. My strategy was to subvert the event. The house that was not even known to the experts in Vienna had to become a Wittgenstein Forum.
On the weekend I informed the international press and a large number of journalists, writers and architects. Taking it into my own hands, I invited them to the meeting so that they could see the unique interior of the house for themselves. Stonborough and Pötschner were both surprised and irritated by the many unwanted guests. The strategy was successful. The quality and striking aesthetics of the building convinced everyone present. Thus, the blind denial of historical facts and aesthetic quality came to end on this day.

On June 21, 1971, it was clear to me that the demolition of the Wittgenstein House had been prevented. It had taken me two years to achieve my goal.

Working drawing, November 15, 1926. Scale 1:50

The building permit drawings (scale 1:100), which were signed by both Wittgenstein and Engelmann, are preserved in the Plan and Document Archives of the City of Vienna. Later plans still in existence (for the construction of a lift shaft or for adaptations) were signed by Wittgenstein alone. Apart from Engelmann's sketchbook (May 1926) no further sketches, no correspondence and no detail drawings from the planning and construction period, which extended from summer of 1926 to autumn of 1928, appear to exist.

This makes the copy of the working drawing still in existence all the more important. In the working drawing the dimensions refer to the unplastered masonry. The building permit drawing is dimensioned using architectural dimensions (i.e., plaster surface to plaster surface). In both plans the spaces and dimensions are, with a few minor exceptions, identical. The working drawing illustrates and describes in a far more concrete way than the building permit drawing the technical and aesthetic complexity of the house as thought through by Wittgenstein from the proportions down to the details. This plan reveals Wittgenstein's intellect and depicts his method.

The building is a compact and complex composition. Nothing can be detached from it or altered. The symmetries and asymmetrical shifts flow into each other and refer to each other. They represent a form which, although it is absolute, should be read on a number of levels.

The same applies to the proportions. In this building there is no overall or universally applicable planning grid. Nor are there any indications that a single theory of proportion applies to the entire building. There are, however, numerous connections in terms of dimensions that establish the intended balance and harmony. For example: the dimension between the plastered surfaces of the piers in the hall is 280 cm, the metal doors to the salon are half as wide (140 cm), which also applies to the window-doors leading from the salon onto the terrace (2:1); the window-doors on the other hand are 320 cm high which is two thirds of 480 cm, the width of the salon (2:3). The length of the salon is 930 cm, the door to the hall is 310 cm high (3:1).

Wittgenstein's extraordinary architectural achievement is manifested on the main floor of the building. This publication deals exclusively with this layout. (The other floor levels are documented in the relevant specialized literature).

The names used for the various rooms signify their original function and have been taken from the plan documents dating from November of 1926.

In the early thirties, Wittgenstein began pasting photographs in a small pocket album. These are photographs of his family (his mother Leopoldine, his sisters and other relatives), friends (Koder, Pincent, Skinner, Labor, Drobil, Moore), landscapes and places (Norway, Traunsee, Hochreith) and occasions (Christmas on Alleegasse). Some of the photos were trimmed by Wittgenstein and combined with others. The photographs are pasted on the right-hand side, with the verso pages remaining blank. In a purely pictorial language he mounted a multi-layered image of his milieu: without text, dates, notations, captions, page numbers, and without a clear temporal sequence.[1] In this album, which he always carried with him, Wittgenstein pasted eight photographs of the house he had built for his sister Margarethe Stonborough. These photographs were taken by Moritz Nähr after the completion of the building.

[1] The numbers on the right-hand pages were later added by someone else.

Ludwig Wittgenstein's pocket photo album

The small book with blue lines measures 98 x 160 mm, with pasted photographs it is 30 mm thick. Cardboard cover of green synthetic linen with red linen spine.

51 Wittgenstein's pocket photo album (p. 34)

The client: Margarethe Stonborough
The architect: Ludwig Wittgenstein

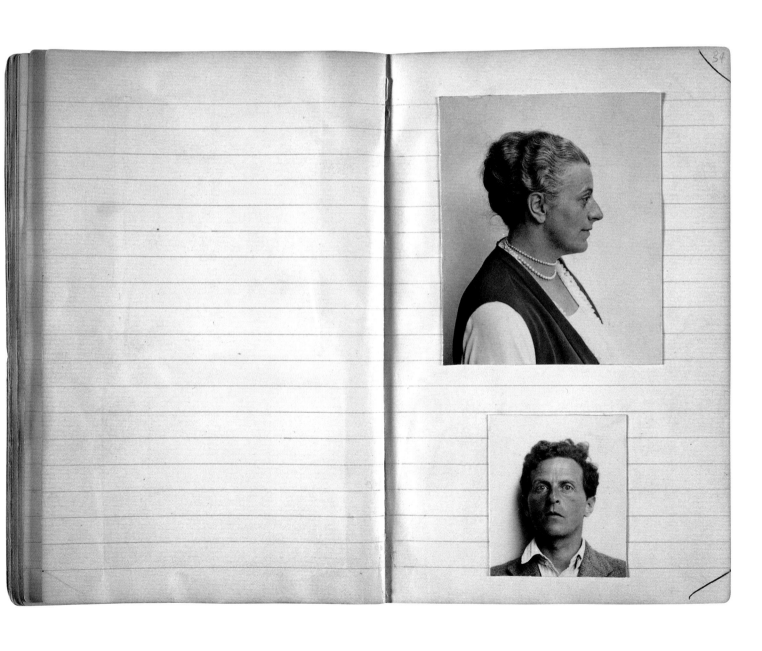

In a letter written in September 1949 to his sister Margarethe,
of which only fragments remain, Wittgenstein mentions the building
on Kundmanngasse, stressing how "enchantingly" Margarethe
had furnished the house. He ended by saying:
"On this matter we understand each other."

53   Pocket photo album (p. 52)

View of the hall after completion. In order to have the figure appear
to stand in the axis of the space, the base had to be shifted somewhat
to the left. Two years later, this copy of an ancient male sculpture
was replaced by the plaster cast of an ancient female torso
with a draped gown in upright position. Correspondingly,
the base was shifted into the axis of the hall.

55 Pocket photo album (p. 53)

The hall after completion in 1928. The photograph
shows the lighting fixture designed by Wittgenstein:
an inverted cone-shaped lamp shade of white silk.
Wittgenstein soon had this lighting fixture removed,
replacing it with a naked light bulb.

56, 57 Pocket photo album (pp. 19 and 17)

Two views of the house from the garden with old trees.
The driveway slopes upward from the Kundmanngasse
to the gravel-covered forecourt.

58 Aerial view, 1959

The immediate surroundings of the Wittgenstein House have been drastically altered since 1976. The main entrance was moved from Kundmanngasse to Parkgasse. A geometric design of steps made out of concrete lead up to the concrete forecourt, originally covered with gravel. The squares on the plan depict the lighting elements of the auditorium (seating 250 people) which was constructed under the former garden in 1976.

A fourteen-story high-rise was originally planned to be located on the very site of the Wittgenstein House after its demolition. In 1976, this skyscraper (marked as dark-gray surface) was built in the southwestern part of the former garden. It is set apart from the Wittgenstein House by a pathway with access to underground parking, which is only twelve meters wide.

Both of the terraces leading down the garden played a significant role for the Wittgenstein House. The high-rise, as well as the underground auditorium, have disrupted this relation house—terrace—garden. Due to the auditorium, the garden level had to be raised by approximately one meter. Northeast terrace and garden are no longer joined. On the other side of the house the terrace itself has been turned into the boundary of the lot, eliminating the garden area completely. The high-rise has been built as close to the Wittgenstein House as possible. Cantelever beams from the entrance of the skyscraper jut over to the Wittgenstein House in an agressive, menacing way. City silhouette as a silent indictment.

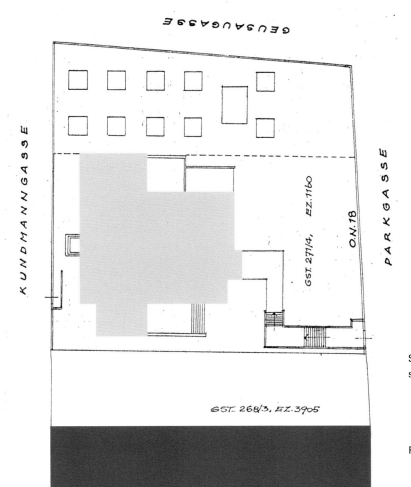

Site plan for alterations, submitted December 12, 1975

Fourteen-story skyscraper

The original layout of rooms in the three-story mansion corresponded to the client's life style. On the main floor there were the reception rooms (salon and dining room) with access from the hall, the husband's study (living room), the living quarters of Margarethe Stonborough (sitting room/bedroom), a servant's room and the (hardly ever used) breakfast room. On the upper two floors were the children's rooms and servants' quarters, guestrooms and the husband's apartment. In 1928, the following staff lived and worked in the house: a cook, two girls who assisted her in the kitchen, three maids, a secretary, a lady's maid, a governess, a chauffeur. A seamstress worked at the house, but lived elsewhere. Heinrich Postl, originally switchboard operator and doorman, worked and lived in the newly built gate-house next to the driveway entrance. Another servant and his wife occupied an older converted building, which served as the site office during construction.

In December 1975, the former People's Republic of Bulgaria purchased the mansion that had been unoccupied since 1971. The building was renovated and the interior altered to conform with the new use. Larger rooms were created to accommodate lectures, concerts and exhibitions. Since then the Wittgenstein House has served as the Cultural Institute of the Bulgarian Embassy (see History, pp. 36–37).

61   Main elevation facing Parkgasse

The main entrance is as an architectural element by itself, projecting 90 centimeters from from the southeast facade. As such, it is clearly an independent entrance facade. The door opening is 162 cm wide and 292 cm high. The areas of wall on either side are 104 cm wide; the surface above the door is 132 cm high. These proportions create a balanced composition of surfaces. Originally, a light bulb hanging from an arm circa twenty centimeters long was positioned above the door.

Main entrance. Original state (photo 1972)

The hall's central staircase may well have been inspired by the Wittgenstein family palais on Alleegasse. But it is not just a formal stylistic variation. It is of a different quality. It is radically new in its spatial composition, in its sense of space and in terms of its spatial effect. This is the essence of Wittgenstein's extraordinary achievement.

The hall is the third room in what can be described as a ceremonial entrance which is composed of an *Eingang* (entrance) extended somewhat along the axis of entry, a second, completely square *Vorraum* (vestibule), in which only the joints between the floor slabs indicate

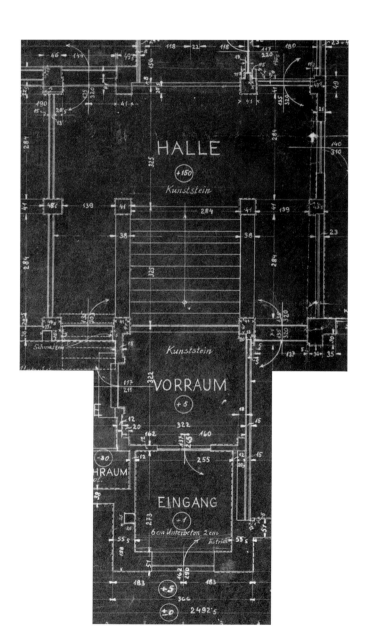

63 View toward space of entrance passage

64 Working drawing, November 15, 1926 (detail). Entrance passage

Hall (650 x 685 cm)

Vestibule (322 x 322 cm)

Entrance (273 x 255 cm)

65 View from the entrance toward the hall

the direction to the hall itself, which is reached via a half-story staircase. This axis is re-echoed in the hall ceiling by two beams, projecting a mere four centimeters below the plane of the ceiling. If these two linear elements were clearly defined beams, strongly indicating a primary direction, the hall's ambivalent character, namely that of a directional/non-directional joint-like center, would be lost. Despite their thinness the strips in the ceiling impressively fulfill their function, which is to redefine the scale of the space. The hall has a width of 6.85 m between terrace and wall plane to the salon but is only 6.5 m long, yet it is extended visually to create a space that appears to have sides of equal length.

Although the hall forms a closed entity, it is at the same time open in various directions. It is not open, however, in the usual modernist sense of a dynamically flowing space. The vertical subdivision of the glass panes conveys a certain "severity." Curiously, the hall—which is narrow in terms of scale—is opened up by the doors and the glass wall to the terrace, even when all the doors are closed. The transparent glass doors allow a view through; the translucent glass intimates that the space extends further. Thus, the space is never entirely self-referring.

Length and width have a 1:1 relationship, not in a geometric sense or in terms of technical scale but rather as an aesthetic effect: this results from a complex weave of interlocking elements and parts, indicated directions and references between dimensions.

The architectural structure (columns, half-columns, quarter-columns) is not set off from the infill walls. The white paint applied to the hall after the war forces one to read the walls as planes. In Viennese modernism, Otto Wagner and Josef Hoffmann created spaces made of planes, emphasizing those planes by framing them with ornamental lines. Wittgenstein's concept of space is completely different. Everything is connected to everything else. Transitional areas with manifold meanings define the hall as a space in and of itself and at the same time link it to the adjoining rooms.

In order to create the impression of a completely homogeneous space in the hall, Wittgenstein combined different construction methods and materials (ferrous concrete, tamped concrete, brickwork walls). In the load-bearing structure not all of the columns and half columns

67 Floor plan of the hall with elevations

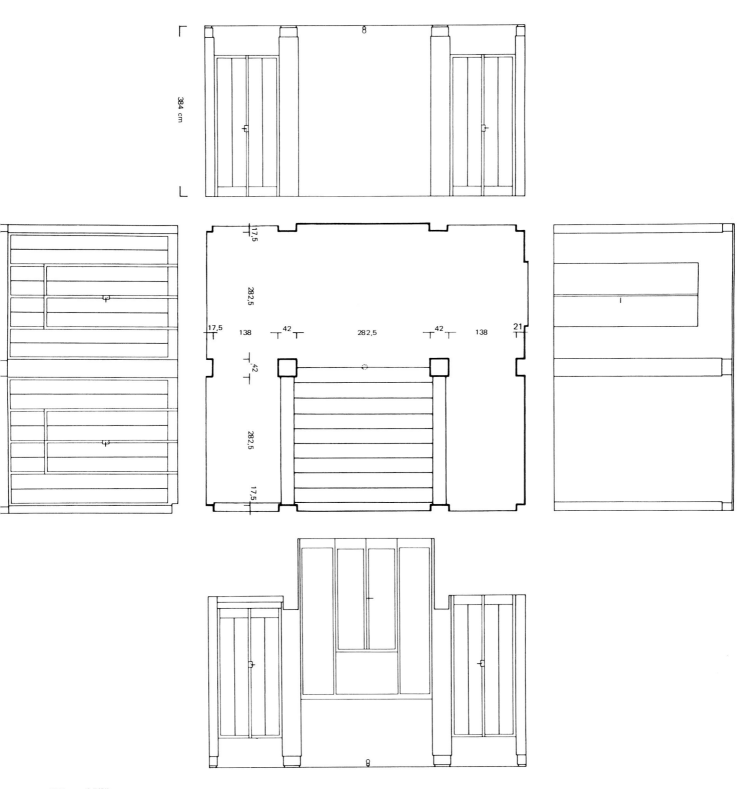

are part of the same structural system. Similarly, he employed walls of different thickness where he found it necessary. The quarter piers in the corner are joint-like transitional elements just as the double glass doors form joint-like connections to the surrounding rooms. Although the dimensions of the hall are modest, the effect is generous, almost monumental. It is a powerful spatial gesture that is closed yet open at the same time. Each element has more than a single meaning. The language used here can be understood on different levels. One space can be read in a variety of ways.

Hall. View toward the entrance. To the left double doors to the living room

All the glass doors leading from the corners of the hall to the adjoining rooms are twin pairs of doors (i.e. four door leaves in all) with one exception: the connecting door to the breakfast room, which lies five steps higher than the hall, consists of a single pair of glass doors which, for reasons of symmetry, stands on the first step. Both leaves of this door open into the hall. The pairs of double doors between hall and dining room, hall and staircase and hall and living room are, perhaps, intended to reduce the transmission of noise between the rooms. But it seems likely that the primary consideration was a design issue: the internal

Hall. Glass wall opening to the southwest terrace

door elements with their doubled vertical composition should differ as little as possible from the climatically necessary inner and outer glazed windows and window doors leading onto the terrace. This unifying design of doors and windows creates a strong sense of calm in the central layout.

The connection between hall and living room consists of two pairs of transparent glass doors whereas in both doors at the opposite end of the hall (one leading to the staircase, one to the dining room) one pair of glass doors is transparent, the other translucent. This combination allows different ways of making translucent and transparent spatial connections between hall and dining room and between hall and staircase. There is a direct visual connection when the transparent doors are closed and the translucent doors are open. When closed the translucent doors separate inside from outside without sealing the interior hermetically as a metal door would do.

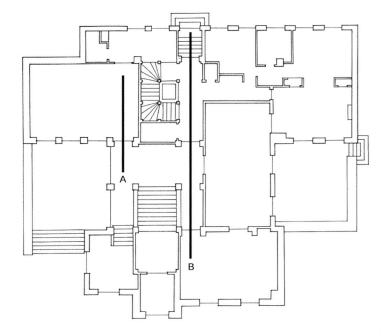

71
A View from the hall into the dining room

72/72a/72b
B View from the living room through the hall toward the staircase and the service entrance

Pair of glazed double doors between the hall and the living room

77 Pair of glazed double doors between the hall and the living room

With these tall, slender double doors Wittgenstein develops a temporary aesthetic image, a series of architectural gestures that make the connections between the spaces both visible and tangible as one moves around the house. The inner pair of leaves of each set of double doors opens into the hall whereas the other pair opens into an adjoining space. These are two gestures pointing in opposite directions: leaving a space and entering a space. If both pairs of double doors are completely open, a temporary architecture of transition, a kind of processional architecture, is created.

Thus, Wittgenstein emphasizes, or indeed almost celebrates the short route, in which the temporal sequence of leaving and entering is abolished. The connection, the "joint" becomes an architectural symbol depicting the time of transition and extending the line separating two spaces in the direction of both. When the two pairs of doors are closed, this transitional space is folded back into the wall.

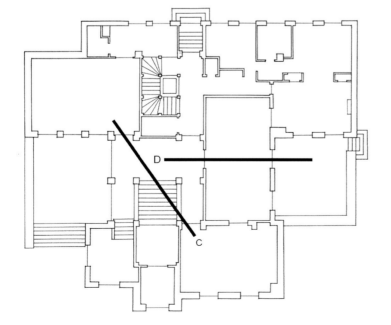

79
C View from the living room through the hall toward the dining room

80/80a/80b
D View from the hall, looking toward the door into the salon, the salon itself and on to the terrace

81 Plain metal door between hall and salon

The connection between hall and salon has a critical significance in the overall spatial concept. After passing through the hall, guests were received in the salon. To underscore this function, this door contrasts with the others in the hall in terms of dimension and material. It is a two-leaf, plain metal door, ten centimeters lower in height but five centimeters wider than the glazed double doors. Half of the wall opening equals the width of the framing lateral wall plane: both measure seventy centimeters. The same measurement is repeated between door and beam.

All door handles in the hall are mounted at the height of 154.5 cm; the exception is the handle of the door to the salon which is twelve centimeters lower: for this plain metal surface Wittgenstein decided on a measurement of 142.5 cm from the bottom of the door. Even these twelve centimeters are testimony to Wittgenstein's striving for very subtle differentiation and architectural complexity. This door refers in its proportions to the framing symmetrical wall, as opposed to the main entrance door. Both constitute a balanced, harmonious design arrived at in different ways. The plain metal door forms a counterpoint within the architecture of the hall, giving this space a subtle directional emphasis.

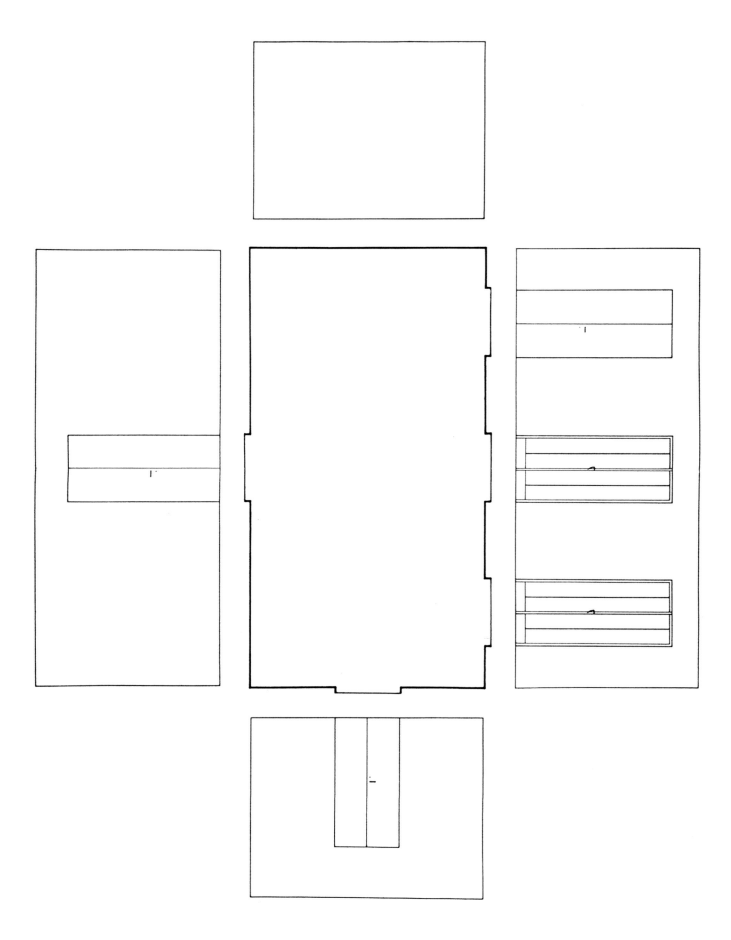

82 Floor plan of the salon with elevations

83 Working drawing, November 15, 1926 (detail). Salon

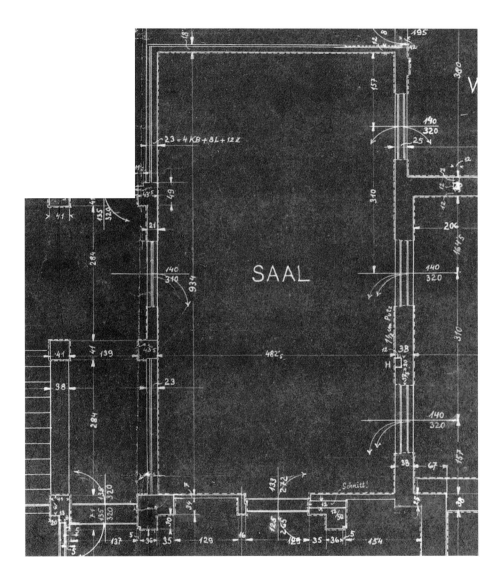

The salon is the most harmonious of all the spaces. Its dignity is reflected in its strict symmetric order. The surface of the opposite wall, which relates axially to the metal door, is articulated by three identical wall openings. As a result, it is read as a single wall although it is actually both an external wall (two window-doors) and an internal wall (full metal door leading to the sitting room/bedroom). It can be represented in numbers as 2:1. Read as a surface the wall is symmetrically defined by the number 3. The openings of the walls on the long axis of the space amount to the numbers 3:1.

Wittgenstein designed the salon as a space resting within itself. The smooth surfaces with their silky sheen are structured only by doors and window-doors. Three 200-watt light bulbs hang from the ceiling as basic lighting. The interplay of finely tuned proportions is the decisive design element in this reductive formal idiom. The dimensions of the door openings relate to wall, space and sense. Wittgenstein had the ceiling of this space lifted by three centimeters after the completion of the building in order to correct the proportions.

Salon in its original state (1972)

In order to create a coherent exhibition/concert space for the Bulgarian Cultural Institute in 1976, the central role that the salon once played in the architectural gestalt of the building was diminished—with the approval of the Vienna Landmarks Preservation Commission. By demolishing the wall to the living room a dynamic modernist space was created that has nothing to do with Wittgenstein's architecture and is opposed to his intentions for the building. Architectural nonsense emerged out of Wittgenstein's sense of space.

Salon after the conversion in 1976

Letter from Paul Engelmann to Hermine Wittgenstein dated January 9, 1932

Dear Miss Wittgenstein,
Your drawings of the rooms in Kundmanngasse have given me indescribable pleasure and I wish to thank you profoundly for them. They are extremely beautiful images. That is your achievement. In addition, one must see here the achievement of your brother and sister. Despite the fact that I had no part in these images, alone the thought that I had something to do with the creation of such beautiful things gives me a certain pleasure. Unfortunately, my participation was more in a negative than a positive sense. At that time, I wanted to make something quite different, something of my own. Now, when your brother's work can be seen in its final form, it is clear how far my own work would have lapsed behind something far better, something which I little understood at the time. Unfortunately, one reaches such awareness only after the event and at the time I was more of a hindrance than a help. Nevertheless, I was involved, if that is something.

87 Salon. Drawing by Hermine Wittgenstein, 1929
View toward double doors between salon and living room

89 Salon. Drawing by Hermine Wittgenstein, 1929
View toward double doors between salon and sitting room/bedroom

Hermine Wittgenstein was Ludwig Wittgenstein's oldest sister. Even though, in Ludwig's words, the house only "suited" his sister Margarethe, Hermine had nothing but the greatest admiration for her brother's exceptional achievement and the quality of the building. Her recollections of her brother and his work as an architect (during the war years she neither saw Ludwig nor set foot in the house), written in the spring of 1945, are one of the few authentic testimonies on the development of Wittgenstein's building. They are just as valuable as they are impressive. The same is true of the drawings that Hermine made in 1929 of the interior at the express wish of her brother Ludwig. They offer a precise depiction that is objectively drawn. The drawings[1] are particularly valuable because they illustrate how Margarethe Stonborough furnished and inhabited the house from 1928 on. (Her family moved into the house in the fall of that year.) Wittgenstein valued his sister's taste and described the style in which she furnished the house as "enchanting." As opposed to the many avant-garde buildings from Wright to Rietveld, Mies van der Rohe and Pierre Chareau, Wittgenstein's architecture is not a stylistic gesamtkunstwerk (total work of art) in which building and furniture complement each other aesthetically. Wittgenstein draws a clear line here. He is only interested in questions of architecture, to which he builds his answer. And this architecture, which is independent of a stylistic period, is in a sense timeless, can be furnished, inhabited, and brought to life with antiques or modern pieces—as long as their quality does justice to Wittgenstein's spaces.

[1] "Mining is now drawing in the salon. From my bed I can hear her moaning and sometimes she comes in here with plenty of smuts around her nose. A consequence of her constantly rubbing her face." (Letter from Margarethe to Ludwig, November 1929)

90 Wittgenstein's pocket photo album (p. 1)
   Sitting room/bedroom, approx. 1930. Marguerite Respinger, Margarethe Stonborough, Primarius Foltanek, Talla Sjögren, Ludwig Wittgenstein, Schönherr-Buchheim, Arvid Sjögren

91 Transition between salon and sitting room/bedroom
   Pair of double doors. Salon side: two full metal doors. Inner side: two glass leaves

Transition between salon and sitting room/bedroom

In Wittgenstein's architecture transitions are just as significant as those in music or choreography. How materials, colors, surfaces, and spaces are delineated, come together, relate to each other, and merge. With the doors Wittgenstein masters an intricate game of varying the interconception of spaces. Metal closes off, while translucence alludes to something beyond, transparent glass is inviting. Transitions, in their material nature are like metaphors of movement. The most unusual transition is the pair of double doors between salon and sitting room/bedroom. By virtue of their materiality they are a rare connection between open (glass) and closed (metal). When in use this pair of double doors offers numerous variants for Margarethe Stonborough's private living area between invitingly open and reclusively closed. When the metal leaves are closed, full acoustic and visual separation is achieved. When the metal doors are open and the glass doors closed, the salon is visually integrated in the more intimate area. A single closed metal leaf signifies something else again. An open single glass leaf is like an open approach whereas when both doors are wide open,[1] salon and sitting room/bedroom merge, creating one space bound together by the two identical window-doors in either space.

[1] The missing original handle on the inner side of the metal door was a ring that could be folded back. It was manufactured especially for this situation. The distance between the two double doors is too small to accommodate a normal door handle. In 1976, a handle Wittgenstein had designed to be fitted horizontally was simply mounted vertically.

Without the wall element between living area and dressing room, which was destroyed in 1976, the proportional system of the sitting room/bedroom (joint plan, window-doors, volume) can no longer be recognized. Margarethe Stonborough slept in the opening of the eighty-centimeter-wide wall element that was accessible from either side. On both sides of the opening, there were mirror doors (passage and closet). Even the fireplace was a crucial element of the strictly symmetric, harmoniously proportioned private living and working area. The fireplace was cast out of the same dark gray, almost black artificial stone as the floor slabs—a jointless, monolithic piece.

94 Temporary reconstruction of the wall element in the sitting room/bedroom for the documentary exhibition put together by Otto Kapfinger and Bernhard Leitner at the Wittgenstein House, September 13–October 29, 1989

95 Fireplace in the sitting room/bedroom, designed by Wittgenstein, destroyed in 1976 (Photo 1972. Pictures and furniture digitally removed)

97   Dining room with closed door to hall (left)
     and closed window-doors to southwest terrace

98   Ludwig Wittgenstein's pocket photo album (p. 51)
     Dining room, approx. 1930

99   Dining room with door opened to hall and
     window-doors opened to southwest terrace

100 Detail from 99

The two terraces are essential elements in Wittgenstein's overall architectural concept. One is adjacent to the hall and the dining room, the other to the salon and the sitting room/bedroom, both on the same level as the spaces they serve. They inspire Wittgenstein to reflect on the transition between inside and outside. In Wittgenstein's building, situated in the middle of an old park, the separation between inside and outside remains clear. This was at the time when modern architecture sought to link inside and outside in a completely new way by means of large glazed walls. (Mies van der Rohe used the largest glass pane available as an expression of his time.) The glass pane that extends nearly floor to ceiling incorporates the terrace in the interior even when the window-doors are closed. When open the double window-doors strongly accentuate the transition between inside and outside, instead of blurring it. Just as the double doors in the interior become temporal spaces of transition when they are open in both directions, a transitional zone, a boundary layer, an intermediate space is created which is both inside and outside. The transition itself is made material.

98

100

103   Dining room with window-doors open to the southwest terrace

Wittgenstein thinks through the movement of transition and then gives it form. The hidden catch that holds the inner and outer door leaves together when open is one of the most brilliant inventions in his architectural work. He did not wish to use hooks, lugs or other forms of fastening to fix these doors. He designed a metal "beak" fixed to the lower frame of the inner leaf and a runner at the same position on the opposite, outer leaf in order to hold the two heavy door leaves together. This "beak" is a cast metal element, a spring plate with a small calotte is screwed into it from below. On the underside of the runner opposite there are six shallow depressions. The "beak" locks into the runner, thereby fixing the doors in one of six possible positions. On examination it was revealed that this "beak catch" actually locks along the entire length of the runner so that it is possible to create a manifold variety of gradual transitions and of different angled configurations of the glass wall. The point bearing of the spring plate with the calotte holds the heavy door leaves together; the "beak catch" can be released as easily as it is fastened.

The various positions of the double doors are like symbols of different connections, different transitions between inside and outside. Wittgenstein plays with variations of giving the space a meaning, of forming the wall. He folds the wall surface to create a glass screen with narrow ventilation slots and modifies it to create, when all the doors are open, a layer of boundary space that is both inside and outside.

104/105/106　Beak-like catch to hold together the inner and outer leaves of all the window-doors opening onto the southwest and northeast terrace.

107 Northeast terrace. Window-door in the salon
The double leaves fixed together to form a narrow ventilation slot

109 Salon. Window-doors folded into a crystalline, glazed screen—
like a rigidly fixed spatial boundary

Between 1926 and 1976, the grounds were entered from Kundmanngasse 19. This was also where the gatehouse built by Wittgenstein and demolished in 1972 once stood. The access route, followed in a gentle curve to the principal entrance, which is on the Parkgasse side of the building. Margarethe Stonborough and her husband drove up to the main entrance door, while the children and staff used a side entrance on Kundmanngasse. This gently curved route winding around the house formed an effective contrast to the severity of the building.

110 View from the southwest terrace through the hall and the salon to the northeast terrace

111 View from the entrance on Kundmanngasse toward the southwest facade of the house with the terrace, around 1930

112 Photo dating from the 1950s, taken from the balcony terrace at second floor level, of the southwest terrace that connects garden and house

113 Approach to the southwest terrace; the doors between the hall and the terrace are open

Initially, Wittgenstein designed lampshades made of white silk which he had mounted on the ceiling to examine the effect they made. They consisted of an inverted cone, fifteen centimeters high, with a base diameter of about fifty centimeters.[1] These light fittings, essentially a geometrically reduced form of chandelier, were replaced after a brief period by naked light bulbs screwed into sockets hung from the ceiling. Only this form of lighting was part of Wittgenstein's architecture. In order to illuminate the spaces for various social uses or more intimate occasions, Margarethe Stonborough used numerous standard lamps and, in the dining room, candlesticks. She decided upon the nuances of the lighting effects in the same way as she decided upon the furnishing of the rooms—to Wittgenstein's great satisfaction. "Both the house and garden are now very pleasant to live in. But you know, the garden is just as much of a challenge as the house and consequently, I cannot find suitable garden furniture for the area beneath the chestnut tree."[2]

[1] Conversation with Heinrich Postl, August 3, 1972
[2] Letter from Margarethe to Ludwig, June 6, 1929

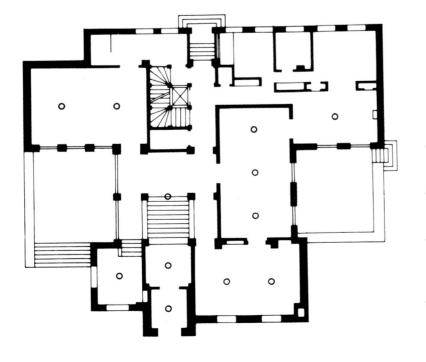

114 Location of light bulbs on the main floor

115 Hall. A 200-watt bulb hangs from the center of the ceiling

116 View across the southwest terrace towards the dining room, early evening

117 View of the dining room and the hall, both lit up

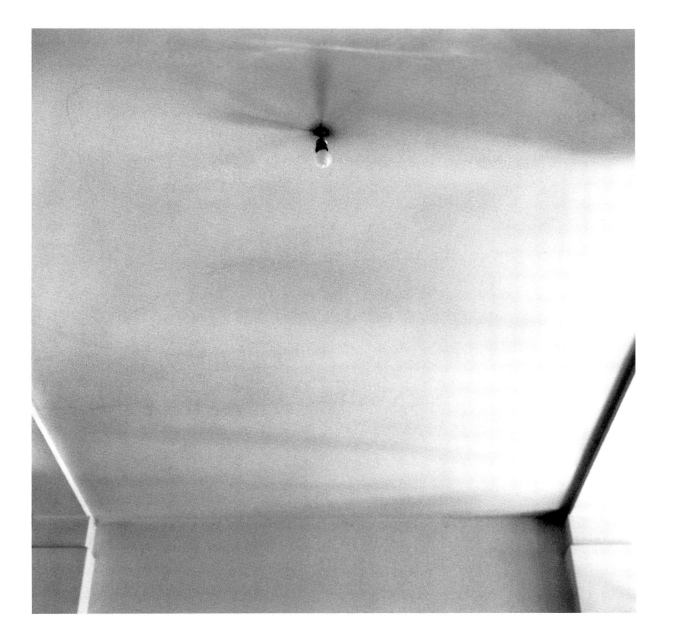

When the lights are switched on, it becomes particularly evident to what extent the building opens up to both the terraces and the garden, how the large openings in the (built) block create a surprising degree of transparency in an architecture that can seem so hermetic. This lighting also reveals the overlapping of vertical frames and mullions that, as one moves, constantly creates new rhythmical patterns of the glazed surfaces during the day inside, at night primarily outside.

View across the terrace toward the salon and the sitting room/bedroom, both lit up inside (Photo 1999)

As far as the conceptual idea and its technical execution are concerned there is barely anything comparable in the history of interior design. In order to close up the sharply defined wall openings containing the window-doors in the evening, Wittgenstein invented a solution that was as ingenious as it was expensive: the metal curtain which, during the day, could be lowered into the basement.

Its proportions alone lend this completely smooth and shiny surface a special appearance. The visible surface of such a curtain is the area of the wall opening, 140 cm wide, 340 cm high.

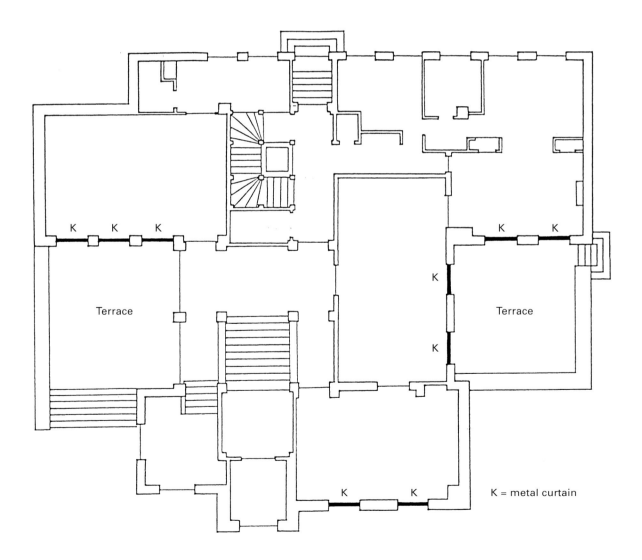

K = metal curtain

The metal curtain certainly served to provide increased security, but more importantly it functioned as a substitute for the usual kind of curtains which Wittgenstein had "forbidden" his sister so as not to distract from the clarity of his architectural language. (Mies van der Rohe, in contrast, did not hesitate to close up his Tugendhat house in the evening with lengths of curtain.) When Mrs. Stonborough retired to bed, the metal curtains were raised. "Weightlessly they floated upwards"—this is how the housekeeper, Heinrich Postl, described the way in which the house was closed up at night. The metal curtain has neither bars, handles nor locking device. Employing technical expertise, logical thought and a radical way of creating form Wittgenstein here arrives at one of the most fascinating aesthetic forms in his architec-

ture. This solution is technically succinct and convincing architectural form. However often one uses it, it remains sensually stirring. A greenish-gray varnished color plane only becomes visible through the interplay between weight and weightlessness.

The "handle": in order to raise the metal curtain weighing around a hundred kilograms Wittgenstein developed a block and tackle system with a precisely calculated counterweight and a lever mechanism that functioned as a "handle." This "handle" consists first of a twelve-millimeter hole-like depression located twelve millimeters beneath the cover plate to the curtain that is set flush with the floor. The second element of the "handle" is a seven-millimeter-thick, twenty-millimeter-wide cross bar at the center of the heating grille, which is also flush with the floor and lies in front of the curtain cover plate. The grille measures 141.5 by 15.7 cm. The edge of the frame closer to the window is twelve millimeters wide whereas the edge on the room side has a width of only ten millimeters. It is twenty millimeters thick. This floor element with dimensions that are finely attuned to its position in the space is not screwed down, its weight alone "secures" it in its setting. Aesthetically, it is an entity in itself. But like all elements in Wittgenstein's architecture the heating grille relates through its dimensions and form to, and is interlocked with, other elements. The third part of the "handle" is a rod designed by Wittgenstein with a hooked point. This rod, which is the lever arm, is inserted into the hollow, the cross bar functioning as fulcrum and is used to raise the metal curtain. (Unfortunately, details of the length, form and material of Wittgenstein's lever arm no longer exist.)

120/120a/120b/120c
Metal curtains in the living room

121
Cover plate to the central metal curtain in the dining room that has been lowered into the basement. In this case, exceptionally, the hole is the "handle," without a fulcrum in the grille.

123
(above) Brass metal grille to the heating duct in front of the window doors

(below) Cover plate of the lowered metal curtain. Brass heating grille, at the center is the cross bar which forms the fulcrum for the lever "handle"

124 The counterweight is lowered, the metal curtain has been raised.

125 The metal curtain with its extended foot piece has been lowered into the wall niche. The counterweight rises up half the metal curtain's track.

The block and tackle

On either side of the upper wall opening in the basement a steel cable fitted to a bracket leads first over a pulley mounted on the counterweight, then back up to a second pulley, which is swiveled through ninety degrees and mounted on the bracket, and over this pulley to a fixing point on the foot-like extension piece to the curtain. A container filled with small metal pieces fixed to the top of the counterweight allows fine adjustment of the weights.

The guide wheels to the curtain on either side (with a profile which tapers to a point) run in V-shaped tracks set into the stuccolustro render. The contact is made only along a line—to ensure a minimum of frictional loss.

The exact adjustment ensures that metal curtain and counterweight are in a state of perfect balance.

Metal is regarded as a metaphor for both heaviness and precision, it represents legible, tangible and perceptible weight. By inserting the lever arm and exercising a minimum of force the metal curtain "floats weightlessly upwards." Wittgenstein's aesthetic of weightlessness is the result of combining his demand for exactitude and precision, which could only be achieved by working with metal, and his comprehension of the laws of mechanics.

The metal curtain's inner side is all color and proportion. Not a single screw or angle iron distracts from the tension between width and height. It is an absolute surface designed to close up the space and close out the night. It represents something never achieved, and indeed never previously attempted, in the history of architecture. When the three curtains in the dining room are raised from their housing, a highly unusual and new kind of architectural wall paneling is created.

Metal curtain in the dining room

*It is obvious that there is no relation of "existence"
between color and the place in which it "exists."
There is no intermediary element
between color and space.*

Color and space saturate each other.

*And the way they permeate each other constitutes
the visual field.*

Wittgenstein's handwriting
(Original size)

Manuscript: *I. Band Philosophische Bemerkungen*
(WA1.15.2-4)
Österreichische Nationalbibliothek, Vienna

In Wittgenstein's architecture colors have a fundamental significance that is decisive for the spatial quality. The Wittgenstein House is a house of color.

Walls, floors and doors formed a harmonious composition of colors. Everything had a sheen. The metal doors with their varnished surfaces were reflected in the highly polished artificial stone flooring. ("It is difficult to say what the gray of the metal doors was like, it was much lighter, as the color had become darker over the course of time. I had the feeling that it was a light gray mixed with a bit of green."[1]) The walls and the ceilings of the rooms surrounding the hall are covered with the silky sheen of light ochre stuccolustro with some red added. The sunlight circling the building made the smooth walls and floors gleam. Dematerialization and dissolution of material weight, material severity and material boundaries was the result. The light expands the scale of the space—special sensuality that is foreign to classical modernism.

Here once again Wittgenstein refers to a tradition—a tradition of Viennese interiors—and makes something new out of it. Repeatedly, and not just in the field of architecture, he borrows models that he seeks to surpass, as he himself describes. Hard stuccolustro walls with a coloring that can be subtly adjusted to suit any aesthetic scheme are important elements in the design of official spaces in public buildings of the late nineteenth and early twentieth century in Vienna. Theophil Hansen's Parliament and Otto Wagner's Postsparkasse (Postal Savings Bank) are two impressive examples. Stuccolustro is a durable material that conveys a certain dignity. Wittgenstein wanted to give his architecture this ennobling quality. The artificiality of this material (as opposed to Loos' marble cladding, for instance) allows fine nuances in the color of wall and space. In addition, the hardness of the material enabled him to demand millimeter-sharp edges. The application of large areas of wet stuccolustro presented a great challenge. The entire surface had to be applied without joints, in one single step. The extremely expensive and complicated process of achieving an absolutely smooth surface was justified for Wittgenstein by the aesthetic result—of ultimate classical beauty. The same applies to the metal door, the metal curtain, the stone slabs, and the radiator.

[1] Letter from Heinrich Postl to the author, September 30, 1972

After the war all rooms on the main floor were painted white. This uniform coat of white makes the house appear more conventional. On the other hand it also allows the house to be misread as functionalist and modern, which was neither Wittgenstein's nor the client's intention. The neutral, cool white of the walls inspired Otl Aicher to give the following interpretation of the house in 1987: "The guests appear in front of white walls, the hosts and their guests, their personalities, their silhouettes, their faces and gestures are accentuated against the backdrop of white walls. In addition, there is the fact that only white space has light. Light as an autonomous quality. In colored space it is swallowed by the color. Only in white space does light retain its intrinsic quality." (Otl Aicher. *analog und digital*. Berlin 1991.) A misunderstanding. In the field of New Building (Neues Bauen) white is seen as representing rationality, functionality, hygiene. The opposite was the case in Wittgenstein's non-white architecture. The polished and varnished surfaces were receptive to light. By virtue of their smoothness and radiance they are sensuous in a haptic way. Walls covered with white paint are non-sensuous in a haptic way. When the house was converted in 1976, all of the door leaves and door frames were given a coat of dull brown-green paint. They lost their character. The light is swallowed instead of being reflected back into the room.

The highly polished, almost black artificial stone flooring dissolves the density of the material, while the heavy metal doors negate their real weight by their light green-gray varnish and their weightless movement. The almost abstract spaces become animated by the gleam of colored walls. In lieu of detached objectivity there is "ascetic-sensuous warmth" resulting from material and color.

131 Wittgenstein's color composition in the salon (reconstruction)

Floor: dark gray, almost black artificial stone slabs, polished (original state)

Metal doors: originally light gray mixed with some green. Varnished surface. The original shade (slightly darkened by time) can still be seen on one of the surviving mirror doors and on the metal curtains in the basement despite a layer of dirt.

Salon wall: light ochre, yellowish with some red added, stuccolustro with a sheen (surface next to the door leading to the hall, uncovered in 1989)

In 1971, Heinrich Postl pointed out to the author that the original coloring can still be found under the uniform coat of white paint. At the exhibition on the history of the building that was held at the Wittgenstein House in 1989, Otto Kapfinger and the author not only reconstructed the walls that had been demolished but uncovered the original wall surface in the hall, salon, and staircase in several places.

Until the restoration of the Wittgenstein House is carried out these exposed areas remain the only indication that the original aesthetic effect of the building was that of a gleaming colorfulness.

132   Stucculustro surface in the salon, uncovered in 1989

133   Salon. Color sketch (approximation) View of the wall with double doors to the living room (door handle missing). Wall demolished in 1976

Stone renders have been used on extremely exposed external wall surfaces since the turn of the century, frequently as a substitute for natural stone. They offer a wide range of design possibilities, can be worked in much in the same way as stone and can be used to create large homogeneous surfaces without joints. In addition, they are considerably harder than ready mix plasters. In the Wittgenstein House the artificial stone floor slabs link hall and salon in terms of color whereas the hall with its stone render was deliberately set apart from the surrounding spaces with their light ochre, yellowish-reddish stuccolustro walls. This emphasized the hall's dual function as a space that is both inside and outside, an internal space at rest within itself that is at the same time an outside space for the surrounding rooms.

After the war the hall, like all the other spaces, was covered with a layer of white paint. This uniform white coat blurs the hall's significance as the central joint in Wittgenstein's layout, originally emphasized by different coloring and surface treatment. Furthermore, the white paint conveys the impression of an architecture made up of planes. In its original state the hall must have appeared much more as a homogeneous, three-dimensional architecture that is not based on a (modernist) hierarchy of load-bearing structure and (non load-bearing) infill. The hall had a completely different appearance with the original stone render.

134 Hall. Color sketch (approximation)

View through the hall (gray stone render) to the originally light green-gray metal door and into the salon with walls of light ochre struccolustro

On the left-hand side next to the door, the uncovered area with the original color can be seen.

135 Hall. Area of stone render surface exposed in 1989

The floor in Wittgenstein's architecture is an extraordinary achievement that is both highly original and impressive: no modernist architect thought out and solved this important aspect of architecture in such a radical way. Wittgenstein designed artificial stone slabs as rectangles of various proportions. He could not accept a modular system using grid sizes available on the market. For Wittgenstein's spatial layout a single floor grid extending throughout the main level would have been impossible, as only a very small grid could suit the different proportions of the spaces. Wittgenstein, however, wanted generous, rhythmically calm dimensions, he wanted a particular character with regard to material and space that is created by using large, weighty slabs. Size and proportion of the slabs, the pattern of the joints and their fine network of lines refer in various symmetrical systems to doors, windows and walls. In this way he connects verticals and horizontals in space to create a homogeneous entity.

The highly polished terrazzo floor with its dark, almost black particles was divided into slabs of different sizes and proportions with extremely thin joints. In each case the slabs were adapted to suit the specific space in which they were laid. The surface of the terrazzo is made of crushed limestone particles and a silicate containing pyrite, the maximum particle size being less than one millimeter. The binder is white cement with a small amount of trass. The artificial stone slabs (of different sizes) were cast directly on site. Starting from a wall surface, the sides of one completed slab formed the shuttering for the next slab, which could serve to explain the extremely thin joints.

Beneath the floor there is piping for a hypocaustic heating system which, ideally, requires slabs of minimal thickness. This thickness, which is around only six centimeters for slabs ranging in size between 90 and 105 cm, was achieved by using expanded metal reinforcement. Not a single slab has broken since they were cast.[1]

[1] I am indebted for the technical information on the materials and the detailing of stuccolustro, stone render and artificial stone flooring to D. I. Karl Neubarth, Office of Landmarks Preservation Vienna, Department for Restoration and Conservation.

141 Wittgenstein's joint plan (Hall, salon, dining room)

In one direction the size of the slabs matches, in principle, the distance between the beams of the basement ceiling. The second dimension of the rectangular slabs is, in each case, derived from the space in which they are laid and from the symmetry of its doors and windows. Wittgenstein also uses them to indicate movement and orientation. There are no square slabs. The grid of joints stretches between the walls of each individual space. Each space has its own symmetrical order. Throughout the entire main floor the nets of the spaces are interconnected to create a unified surface by joint or bridge-like pieces set in the door openings. In addition, the subtly diversified joint plan of the overall layout becomes an architectural and aesthetic unity by virtue of its color, a highly polished dark gray, almost black surface. The dimensions of the floor slabs are appropriate for each individual space and yet the entire floor is only a single gesture of Wittgenstein's architecture.

The "free dimensioning" and the deliberate selection of specific proportions for a particular space contradict any modular concept of architecture. But the aesthetic impression of order has its roots in these so-called deviations. This refined and technically sophisticated artificial stone flooring with its razor sharp lines and various systems of proportions contributes decisively to the complexity of Wittgenstein's architecture.

The fact that the artificial stone slabs were cast and finished on site allowed Wittgenstein's abstract joint logic to become material form. To a superficial glance all floor slabs in the spaces surrounding the hall appear the same. However, a large number of sizes is used

Drawings pp. 141–152: B. L.

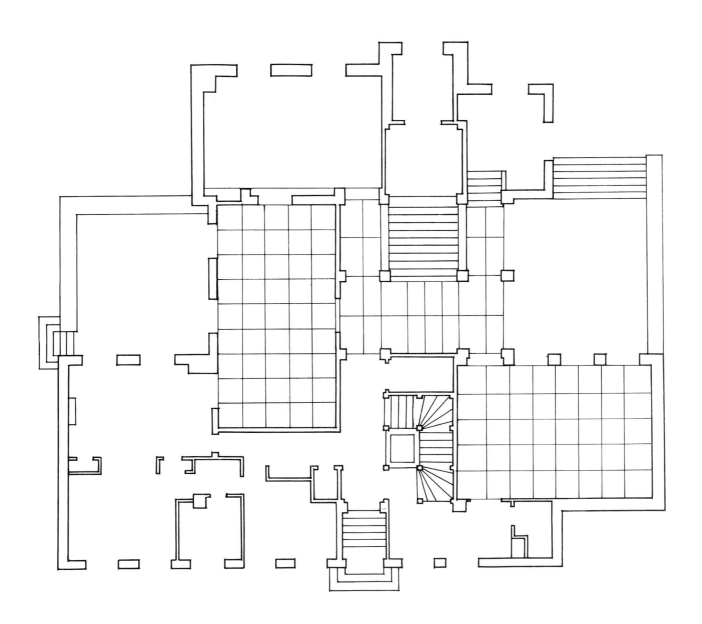

differing only by a few centimeters. Above all, there are numerous corner situations, i.e. rectangular slabs with cutout corners. This meant that it was necessary to draw up and prepare for casting on site a great number of individual pieces. A very difficult, time consuming and expensive procedure. This technique, however, gave Wittgenstein the freedom to create a floor that was both harmonious-generous and precise for a specific task: he extended slabs in a certain direction, designed joint-like slabs in transitional areas, designed grids with broader

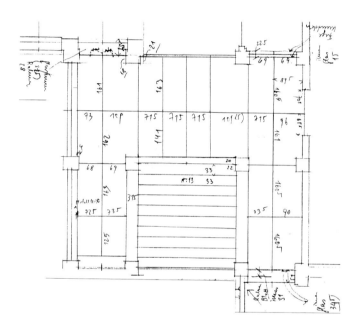

142   Survey of the hall with dimensions

143   Part of main floor with joint plan
      The measurements are the visible dimensions
      of the artificial stone slabs.

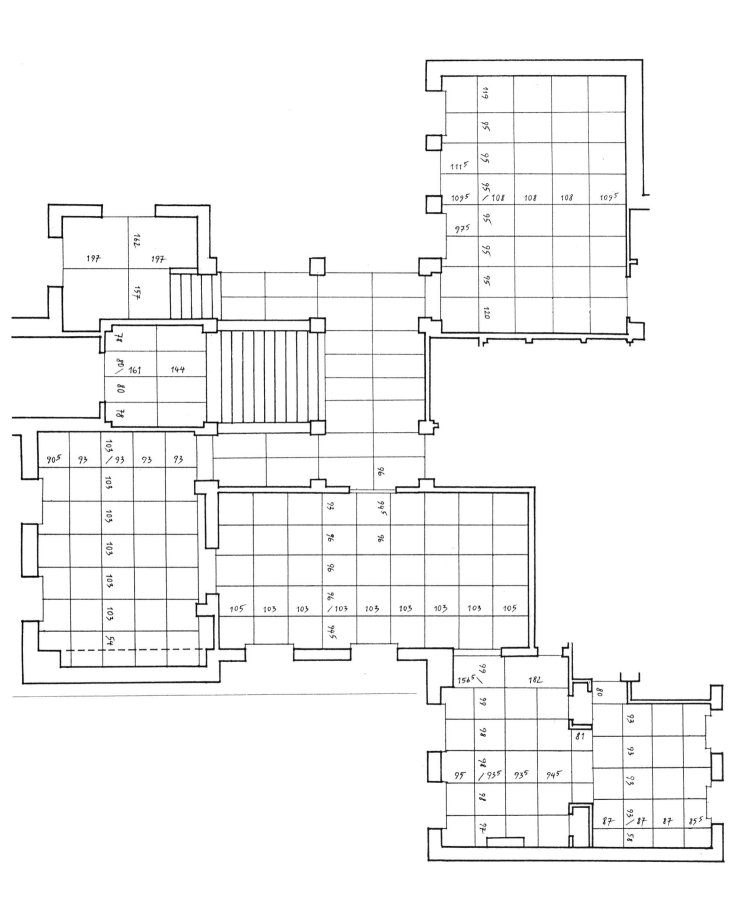

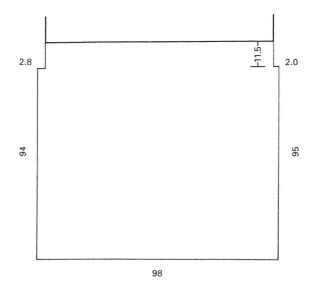

edge slabs thus avoiding leftover pieces at the wall, responded to constructional tolerances, and adapted corner slabs to incorporate the heating grilles. The artificial stone slabs were laid directly against the unplastered walls, the 1.5 or 2 cm of render ends on the slab. A sharp line in space, a precise edge, a precise delineation of space. There are no baseboards concealing the junction of floor and wall, nor could there be any.

144   Stone floor in the sitting room/bedroom. Slab dimensions between the two window-doors

145   Living room. Floor slab with corner detail around a heating grille. No small residual pieces

146 Joint plan, wall openings, heating ducts

Living room. Two windows onto the garden. Two heating ducts

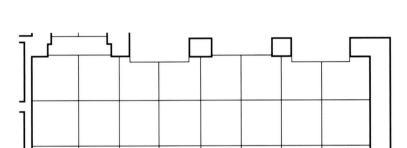

Dining room. Door to the hall, three window-doors onto the southwest terrace. Two heating ducts

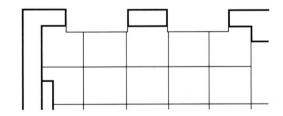

Sitting room/bedroom. Two window-doors. Two heating ducts

Salon. Door to the sitting room/bedroom, two window-doors onto the northeast terrace. Two heating ducts

147 (above) Living room

(below) Transition from hall to salon. Narrow "bridge" between the two joint grids. The joint grid in the salon is symmetrical within itself but, like the entire space of the salon, it is shifted six centimeters to the left of the door axis.

146

Although the dimensions of the slabs at the edge of a grid differ from those at the center, the grid as a whole gives the impression of a regular symmetrical order. Areas cut out of the slabs, for instance, to incorporate the heating grilles do not distract from the system of proportions of a particular grid. The grid remains intact. The configuration of the floor slabs in the four spaces sketched below reveal a calm rhythm of proportions: 5:7, 5:9, 4:5, 5:8. (Two of these could also be read as a consonance: major third 4:5, minor sixth 5:8.)

Dimension and direction of floor slabs are used by Wittgenstein to add a further quality to the sense of space. The vestibule between the entrance space and the hall is square. (The glass wall between the vestibule and the hall is placed on the first step that is extended into the vestibule. The glass wall defines the square, not the floor.) The fine lines of the floor orient the square towards the hall. The joint plan is part of the entrance ritual.

The sitting room/bedroom is entered from the salon through a transitional space which is delineated only in the floor. With the floor joint plan alone Wittgenstein ascribes this barely perceptible "in-between space" to Margarethe Stonborough's intimate living and working area, a harmoniously dimensioned space symmetrical within itself: wall niche, mirror doors, fireplace, window-doors onto the terrace, joint plan.

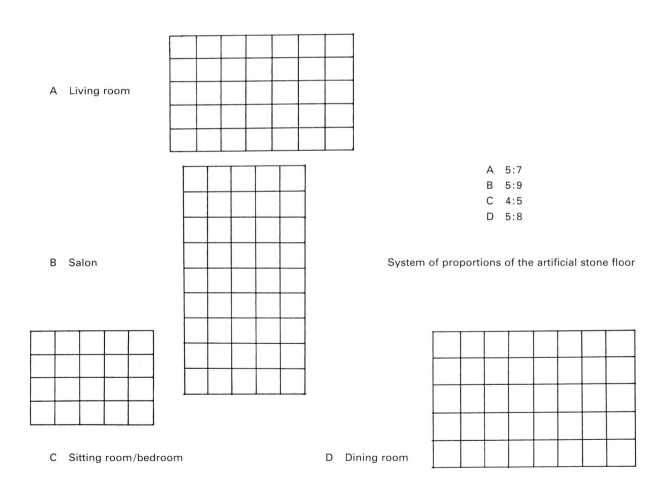

A Living room

B Salon

C Sitting room/bedroom

D Dining room

A 5:7
B 5:9
C 4:5
D 5:8

System of proportions of the artificial stone floor

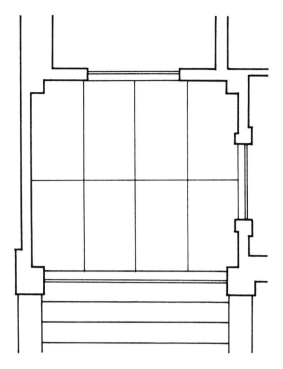

Square vestibule with joint plan oriented towards the hall

Symmetrical joint plan in the sitting room/bedroom
The double sized floor slabs indicate a zone of transition.

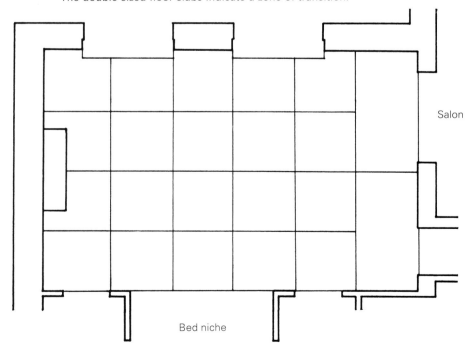

Salon

Bed niche

The route taken by guests leads from the vestibule up the stairs, turning right to the metal door leading into the salon. Despite the strictly symmetrical structure of the hall Wittgenstein underlines this direction in the joint plan by placing a wider slab on the right. After the last step one is subtly invited to turn right.

150   Hall. Wide floor slab on the right-hand, upper end
      of the half-story staircase

151   Hall. Narrow floor slab at the left-hand, upper end
      of the half-story staircase

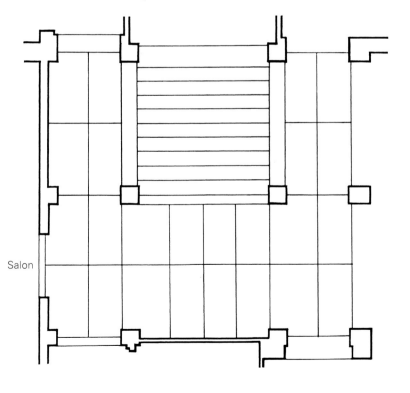

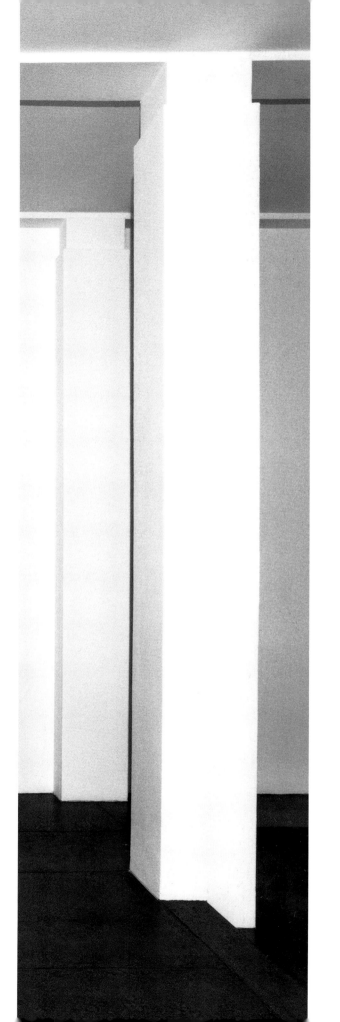

In the construction of the house twelve piers made of ferrous concrete, tamped concrete and brickwork define the hall. They are not equal elements in a single structural load-bearing system. With the exception of the two free standing piers, in each case only a part of a pier (as a pilaster or corner pier) contributes to the strictly symmetrical appearance of the hall. This "new" architectural structure (carved out of the twelve pier-structure) has the effect of a geometrically static hall that rests within itself. Here the pilaster is not an architectural element applied to a surface. The pilaster is not merely added.

152 Hall. Free-standing pier with recessed capital

Schematic sketch of the architectural structure of the hall. Two piers, six pilasters and four corner piers

153 East corner of the hall with pilaster (pier no. 6) and quarter pier (pier no. 7 of the house structure)

(Circle upper left) At both ends of the glass wall to the terrace a quarter capital sits on a quarter pier which itself forms part of the pilaster that lies between the hall and the outside. The beam that runs above the large area of glazing rests, in a structural sense, upon this pilaster. This beam has the same height as the (somewhat reduced) quarter capital so that in these two corners quarter column and pilaster, internal and external architecture, quarter capital and beam flow into each other. An architectural joint with a number of meanings.

Wittgenstein's architecture, which uses transitions with manifold meanings, does not permit the classical kind of capital that extends beyond the shaft of the column. This particular joint aesthetics can only gain form through a recessed capital.

(Circle below right) The pier marked no. 6 in the working drawings appears in the second vestibule as a quarter pier without a capital. As one enters the hall a composite form of pilaster and two-sided pier (up to the upper edge of the glass surface) develops. In the hall itself pier no. 6 of the structural system of the house appears as a pilaster in the strictly symmetrical architectural structure of the hall.

Working drawing, November 15, 1926 (detail). Hall

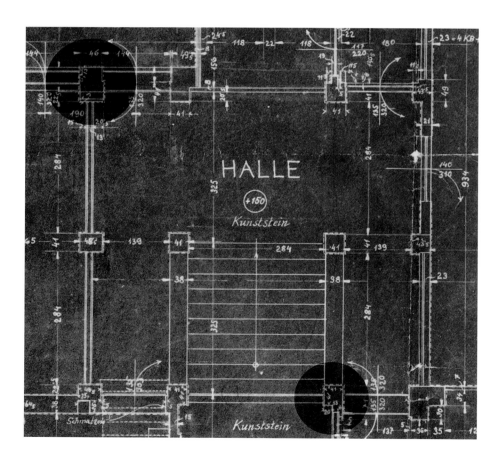

Corner pier in the hall with corner capital and the transition between beam and pier onto the terrace.

24. 10. [1931]
The secret of dimensioning an armchair or a ~~window~~
house is that it changes the perception of the object.
Shorten this one and it appears to be a continuation of this part,
lengthen it and it appears to be a completely autonomous part.
Make it stronger and it appears to support something else,
make it weaker and it appears to be appended to the other, etc.
It is not the gradual (~~quantitative~~) difference in length that really matters,
but the qualitative aspect of perception.

Wittgenstein's handwriting
(Original size)

Ludwig Wittgenstein. *Denkbewegungen:*
Tagebücher 1930–1932/1936–1937. Innsbruck 1997.

24.10.

Das Geheimnis der Dimension eines Teiles oder eines ganzen Hauses ist, daß ~~sie die Auffassung des~~ Gegenstandes ~~sich~~ ~~auffassen~~ ~~Sie~~ ändert ~~macht~~. Mache das ~~kürzer~~ + es sieht aus wie eine Fortsetzung dieses Teiles, mache es länger + es sieht aus wie ein ganz unabhängiger Teil. Mache es stärker + das Andere scheint sich darauf zu stützen, mache es schwächer und es scheint am Andern zu hängen, etc.

Nicht der graduelle (quantitative) Unterschied der Länge ist es eigentlich, worauf es ankommt, sondern der qualitative der Auffassung.

The staircase represents a decisive constructional idea introduced by Wittgenstein in the later planning phase. It is a freestanding, four-story construction with twelve reinforced concrete columns. The entire circulation and multifunctional organization of the house is contained in this idea. The elevator shaft at the center is separated from the steps merely by glass. As a result, the working parts of the elevator remain visible. The elevator is aesthetically incorporated in the private realm of the house.

The surface of the reinforced concrete frame was originally a yellowish stucco lustro. After the war the staircase was given a white coat of paint. The steps and skirting, which are made of light gray fine grained terrazzo with a polished surface, were laid upon a reinforced concrete stairs slab that is curved in three dimensions. The steps that wind around the elevator shaft meet the piers at a precisely calculated angle.

160 Working drawings November 15, 1926 (details). Staircase with elevator. Main level and first upper floor

161 Glazed elevator shaft with the staircase

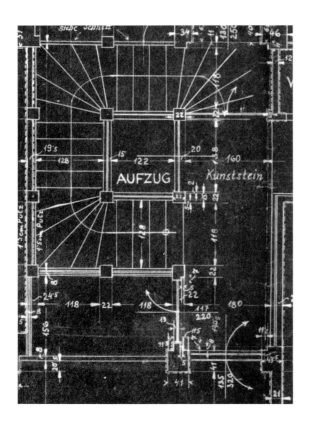
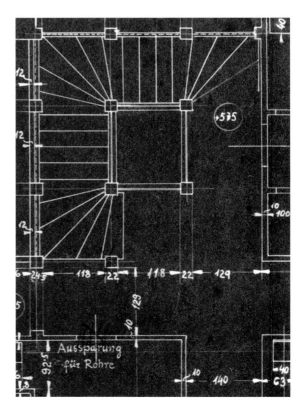

163 Staircase and elevator shaft on the second floor after completion, 1928

For the design of the handrail to the staircase between the basement and the main floor, Wittgenstein took as his starting point the standard staircase handrail, a widely used, tried and tested form fitted to the hand, found in Vienna since the late nineteenth century. A concealed flat metal band recessed in the wood is screwed from below into a rounded wooden profile. This strip of flat metal is fixed at right angles to curved round metal bars anchored in the wall. This model can be found in innumerable Gründerzeit buildings, also in so-called simple tenement buildings. Wittgenstein transformed this handrail to meet his needs. His aim was to adapt more precisely the line along which the hand glides, the way one grips the rail while climbing the stairs, the very act of gripping and ascending. He aimed at a perfectly curved line, as a contrast to the geometrically severe staircase, which wound around the elevator shaft. This could only be achieved at considerable expense.

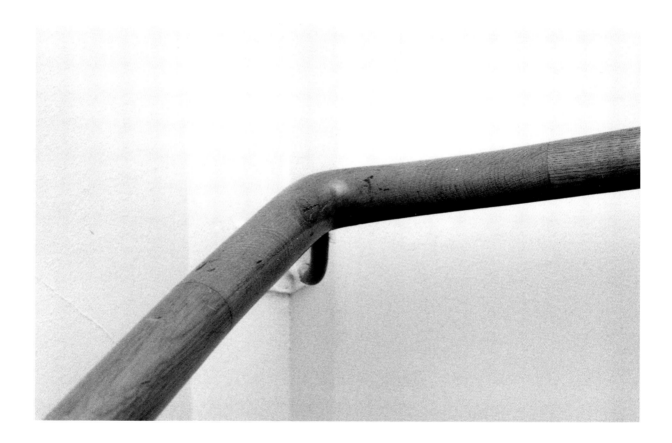

164 Handrail. Cornerpiece bent in convex and concave curves

165 Handrail between basement and ground floor

It is an organic line that starts "from the wall" and with a similar gesture ends "in the wall." The line of curvature of the wooden handrail is parallel to the upper line of curvature of the wall and the cast concrete soffit above. It is also parallel to the line of curvature of the terrazzo skirting to the steps. The geometric stepping of the staircase is counterpointed by curves (falling/rising) as if depicting the gesture of ascending in a single line. In the corners Wittgenstein curves the round wooden section by ninety degrees, whereby—and here is where the difference lies between his solution and the standard functional solution of a short corner piece in the corners—the angled wooden profile piece is forty centimeters long and is curved twice. One arm makes a concave curve along a length of twenty centimeters and, after the ninety degree angle, is bent in a convex curve along a length of twenty centimeters.

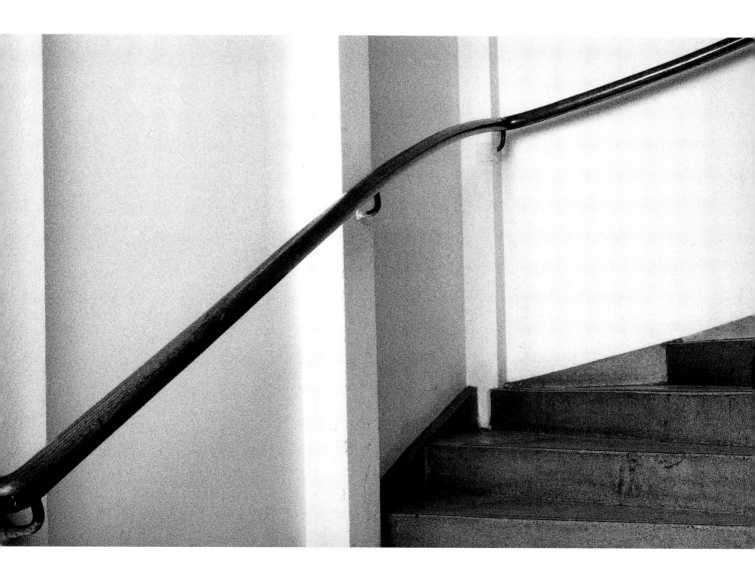

166 Detail of the handrail at the pier to the elevator shaft

167 Staircase. Soffit of the reinforced concrete slab that curves in three dimensions

"I remember, for example, two small, black, cast-iron radiators, which stand in two corresponding corners of a small room. Alone the symmetry of the two black objects in the light room gives a feeling of well-being! The radiators are so flawless in their proportions and in their precise, smooth, slender form that it was not noticeable when Gretl used them after the cold season as a base for one of her beautiful art objects. One day when I was admiring these radiators, Ludwig told me their story and spoke about his own difficulties, and how painfully long it had taken until the precision which constitutes their beauty had been reached. Each of these corner radiators consists of two parts, which stand at precise right angles to each other, and, between them, calculated down to the millimeter, a small space has been left; they rest on legs upon which they had to fit exactly. At first, models were cast, but it soon turned out that the kind of thing Ludwig had in mind could not be cast in Austria. Consequently, ready-made castings for individual parts were imported from abroad, although at first it seemed impossible to achieve with these the kind of precision which Ludwig demanded. Entire sets of pipe sections had to be rejected as unusable, others had to be exactly ground to within half a millimeter. The placing of smooth plugs, too, which were produced in accordance with Ludwig's drawings by a quite different process from the conventional products, caused great difficulties. Under Ludwig's direction experiments often went on into the night until everything was exactly as it should be. As a matter of fact, a whole year passed between the drafting of the seemingly so simple radiators and their delivery. And yet, I consider the time well spent when I think of the perfect form which arose from it."

Hermine Wittgenstein, *Familienerinnerungen*, p. 115.

Radiator in the breakfast room. Originally black unpainted iron, varnished

In Wittgenstein's architecture details cannot be separated from the whole, they are interdependent. Each element of his architecture, such as the floor grille for the heating, the metal door, the dining room wall or the door handle, is aesthetically self-contained. The overall meaning does not result from adding the elements. They reference one another and are closely interlocked in their meanings. It is the spaces on the main level of the house that are of the greatest architectural significance. In this layout one cannot separate the handle from the door, the door from the wall or the wall from the space.

To produce his door handle Wittgenstein employed the cast brass technique standard in Vienna at the time. What is special about Wittgenstein's door handle for the tall metal door and metal and glass doors is that the form on either side of the door leaf is different. This is not a traditional symmetrical door handle. On one side an angled metal bar is fitted directly into the door leaf and is continued as a square section element which has a thread axially drilled into it. On the other side a handle completely different in appearance swings out from the door leaf. It is fitted over the square section bar using a short cylindrical fixing piece. The radius of the cover ring is somewhat smaller than the radius of the cylinder. A screw countersunk in this cover ring axially connects the two handles. This solution is as unusual as it is logical. But in terms of manufacturing it is not a simple solution. Formal simplicity in Wittgenstein's case means aesthetic complexity.

In 1987, Otl Aicher wrote: "Wittgenstein developed the cylindrical door handle, a plain tube bent at a right angle with a hemispherical end."[1] This is not true. Wittgenstein was a master of sensitive geometry. His precise intuition for proportions demanded that, instead of a hemispherical form, the handle should be terminated by a calotte five millimeters high.

[1] Otl Aicher and Robert Kuhn. *Greifen und Griffe.* Cologne 1987.

The handle to the metal doors, clearly designed by Wittgenstein with great attention and effort, must be seen and understood as a single aesthetic element consisting of two entirely different parts. The door handle to the normal wooden doors on the upper floors consists of two identical parts on either side, a handle bent in a tight right angle. In the case of the steel doors no rosette is necessary to connect the metal handle and the metal door leaf. In a metal door the keyhole also has no cover plate.

On the main floor most of the door handles were lost when the empty house became dilapidated between 1972 and 1975. In 1976, they were replaced by handles cast in Bulgaria. These were altered to prevent theft (the axial screw fixing is not visible) and partly for economic reasons. The new handles differ with regard to form and proportion from the original. They are *almost* like the original, which is particularly detrimental to every form of aesthetic reading. The handle has on one side a larger quarter circle curve and on the other a softer, stretched out S-curve. It now appears rather conventional. Seen in Wittgenstein's aesthetic terms it is simply false—although it differs from the original handle only by a few millimeters.

170/171 Handle of a metal door

173/174 Handle of the door between hall and salon. Lost (Photo from 1972 with original setting)

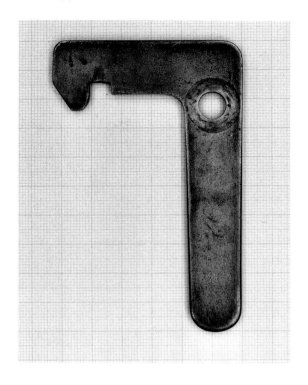

176 Window-door in the dining room

177 Right angled catch (detail) of the external leaf
(cast brass)
Bayonette catch (detail) to the inner leaf
(cast brass)

All the metal works in the house were special, one-off productions, including the door handles and window latches. Only an architectural language so condensed in intellectual and aesthetic terms can justify the aesthetic decision, unique in the history of architecture, to make the door handles in the house of different lengths, depending on the particular function and proportions of the door. The handle to the metal door between the hall and the salon is eight millimeters longer than a similar handle used for a wooden door on the second upper floor.

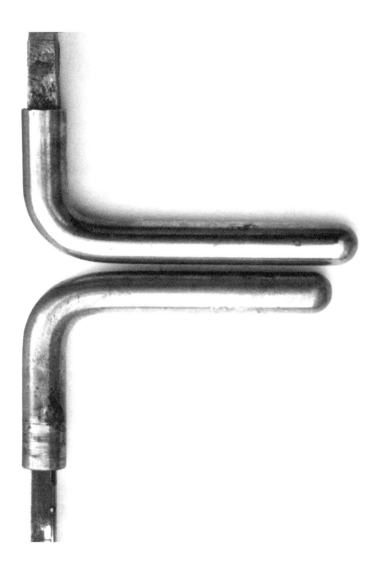

178 Handle of a metal door on the main level in true-to-scale comparison with a handle to a wooden door on the second upper floor

179 Door handle, lock and hinge to the door between the living room and the salon. Destroyed in 1976

Each of the two wings measuring 70 by 310 cm of the metal doors between the hall and the salon weighs circa 150 kg. Wittgenstein supports this weight, which is unusual for a door in a domestic house, on a single point. The upper and lower hinges are merely guiding pins whereas the central hinge is constructed as a sliding/thrust bearing. This applies to all doors and window-doors on the main level.

The hinge has a six-millimeter-thick wall, the bolt measures sixteen millimeters. Wittgenstein reduces the diameter of the bolt twice in order to achieve a particularly balanced movement of the door leaf. The sliding/thrust bearing is a twelve-millimeter-thick disc covered with a thin-walled brass ring.

The heavy metal doors and metal window-doors still move freely today, seventy years later as if they had merely a very light weight or no weight at all. Wittgenstein was able to give the act of opening and shutting heavy metal doors and metal window-doors a kind of weightlessness, negating the weight in motion. This tension is characteristic of Wittgenstein's aesthetics: knowing/also seeing (metal and weight) and feeling/also grasping (weightlessness).

180   Central hinge with the thrust/sliding bearing, full size

181   (left) Central hinge. Bolt for the guiding band and the supporting band

       (right) Door leave in the glass wall to the terrace. The upper and lower hinges are guide hinges. The central hinge is made as single point bearing. Twelve millimeters disc as thrust/sliding bearing

With regard to the question as to how Wittgenstein determined dimensions, Heinrich Postl gave the author the following example in summer 1971. In order to determine the proper height of the horizontal bars in front of a living room window (p. 182) and the distance between them, Wittgenstein had two workers hold the bars for an extremely long time in front of the window. He told them to alter the position from time to time until he, standing in the garden, had found the "right" dimensions that resulted from measuring by eye. In other cases Wittgenstein used numerical proportions or interlocking geometric dimensions and classical symmetrical forms in order to lend his architecture calm and balance. (There is no indication that Wittgenstein based his building on a single theory of proportion).

182 Window of the living room onto the garden

183 South front of the Wittgenstein House with the garden. Original condition (Photo 1971)

185 Wittgenstein's pocket photo album (p. 15)
     View of the house from the corner Parkgasse/Geusaugasse

*Working on philosophy is really working on oneself—
as is often true of working in architecture.
Working on one's own perception, on how one sees things
(and what one demands of them).*

Wittgenstein's handwriting
(Original size)

Manuscript: *VIII. Bemerkungen zur philosophischen Grammatik*
(WA4.124.10)
Österreichische Nationalbibliothek, Vienna

Reading Wittgenstein

To interpret is to think, to do something; seeing is a state.

We find certain things about seeing puzzling, because we do not find the whole business of seeing puzzling enough.

But I do not always have to make judgements, give explanations; often I might only say: "It simply isn't right yet." I am dissatisfied, I go on looking. At last a word comes: "*That's* it!" *Sometimes* I can say why. This is simply what searching, this is what finding, is like here.

The genuineness of an expression cannot be proved; one has to feel it.

Imponderable evidence includes subtleties of glance, of gesture, of tone.

Ask yourself: How does a person learn to get an "eye" for something? And how can this eye be used?
(Ludwig Wittgenstein. *Philosophcal Investigations*. Oxford 1999, pp. 212e, 218e, 228e.)

Perhaps the most important thing in connection with aesthetics is what may be called aethetic reactions, e.g. discontent, disgust, discomfort. The expression of discontent is not the same as the expression of discomfort. The expression of discontent says: "Make it higher ... too low! ... Do something to this."
(Ludwig Wittgenstein. *Lectures and Conversations.* Oxford 1978, p. 13.)

When I see the regularity of a figure that I had not noticed before, then I do see a different figure. Thus I can see IIIIII as a special instance of II II II or of III III or of I IIII I, etc. This only demonstrates that what we see is not as simple as it seems.
(WA2.220.6 – Quoted from Wiener Ausgabe. Followed by page number, followed by note.)

The question is in what sense/the results of/measuring can tell us something about t h a t which we/also/see. (WA2.223.9)

The method of measuring, e.g., of measuring space, is to a certain measurement the same way as the meaning of a sentence is to its truth or falseness. (WA2.228.4)

Today, the danger of wanting to see things in a simpler way than they actually are is often highly overestimated. This danger actually exists to a very high degree in the/phenomenological/investigations of sensory impressions. These are always taken to be m u c h simpler than they/in reality/are. (WA2.233.5)

Space is o n e possibility as it were. It does not consist of several possibilities. (WA2.244.4)

Logic is a geometry of thinking. (WA2.299.4)

Grammar constitutes a mechanism; by allowing certain connections and disallowing others, it acts in the same way as bearings, pilots/guides (and/in general/all pieces) of the mechanism do: it allows certain/specific/movements and thus define the movement/of the parts/. (WA3.19.4)

One cannot understand a sentence detached from a language.
"To express in the same language" means to measure with the same rule.
We can only make comparisons within language. (WA3.96.5,6,7)

Before a combination lock is set to the right combination no force can open the doors. Once the right combination is set, no force is needed to open it. It is difficult for people who have always used doors that can be opened by force (and in proportion to the force applied) to get used to this. (WA3.116.4)

But when the general notion of language dissolves as it were, doesn't philosophy, too, dissolve? No, for its task is not to create a new language but to purge the existing one. (WA3.277.7)

Exactness is an internal relationship. (WA4.56.6)

"Stringent" means clear. (WA4.74.6)

The problem of distinguishing 1 + 1 + 1 + 1 + 1 + 1 + 1 and 1 + 1 + 1 + 1 + 1 + 1 + 1 + 1 is much more important (more fundamental) than it appears to be (at first glance).
It is the difference between a physical and a visual number. (WA4.109.9)

"I cannot see this glass pane, but I can sense it." (WA5.165.4 line)

What makes bright colors b r i g h t ? Does it reside in the concept or in cause and effect? There is no luminous gray. Is this inherent to the concept of gray or is it part of the psychology, that is, of the natural history of gray, and isn't it strange that I don't know this?

"Dark" and "blackish" are not the same concept.

What explains why a dark yellow does not have to be perceived as "blackish", even if we call it dark? The logic of color concepts is simply much more complicated than it might appear to be.

The concepts "matt" and "glossy." If one associates something with "color," which is the property of a point in space, then the concepts matt and glossy do not relate to these color concepts.

If you are not clear about the role of logic in color concepts, begin with the simple case of a yellowish red, for instance. No one doubts that there is such a thing. How do I learn the use of the word "yellowish"? By language games of ordering, for example. I can also learn, in agreement with others, to recognize yellowish and more yellowish red, green, brown, white. In doing so, I take independent steps—as in arithmetic. The task of finding a yellowish blue can be solved by one person by a green-blue, while another person does not understand it. What does this depend on?

The colors (the various colors) do not all have the same connection with *spatial* seeing.

"Transparent" could be likened to "reflective."

Transparency and reflection only exist in the depth dimension. In the depth dimension of a field of vision.
(From: notebook begun on March 24, 1950, MS173)

Selected Bibliography

Aicher, Otl. *analog und digital*. Berlin 1982.

Amendolagine, Francesco and Cacciari, Massimo. *OIKOS da Loos a Wittgenstein*. Rome 1975.

Bering, Kunibert. *Die Rolle der Kunst in der Philosophie Ludwig Wittgensteins – Impuls für die Kunstgeschichte?* Essen 1986.

Gebauer, Gunter et al. *Wien. Kundmanngasse 19*. Munich 1982.

Giacomini, Ugo. *Un opera architettonica di Wittgenstein*. Milan 1965.

Indiana, Gary. "Ludwig Wittgenstein, Architect." In *Art in America*, January 1985.

Kapfinger, Otto. *Haus Wittgenstein. Eine Dokumentation*. Vienna 1984.

Kapfinger, Otto. "Kein Haus der Moderne." In *Biographie, Philosophie, Praxis* vol. 1), Vienna 1989.

Kapfinger, Otto and Leitner, Bernhard, eds. *Wittgenstein Haus. Ein Pressespiegel, Juni/Juli/August 1971*. Vienna 1989.

Leitner, Bernhard. "Wittgenstein's Architecture." In *Artforum*, February 1970.

Leitner, Bernhard. *The Architecture of Ludwig Wittgenstein. A Documentation*. Halifax 1973 (New York 1976).

Leitner, Bernhard. "Das Haus in Bewegung." In *Biographie, Philosophie, Praxis* (vol. 1), Vienna 1989.

McGuinnes, Brian. *Wittgenstein. Familienbriefe*. Vienna 1996.

Nedo, Michael. "Familienähnlichkeit. Philosophie und Praxis." In *Biographie, Philosophie, Praxis* (vol. 1), Vienna 1989.

Nedo, Michael and Ranchetti, Michele, eds. *Wittgenstein. Sein Leben in Bildern und Texten*. Frankfurt am Main 1983.

Schneider, Ursula A., ed. *Paul Engelmann (1891–1965). Architektur. Judentum. Wiener Moderne*. Vienna 1999.

Turnovsky, Jan. *Die Poetik eines Mauervorsprungs*. Brunswick 1987.

Wijdeveld, Paul. *Ludwig Wittgenstein, Architect*. London 1994.

Photo Credits

Bernhard Leitner: pp. 49, 61, 63, 71, 77, 94, 104–107, 109, 110, 115, 117, 118, 121, 123 (above), 123 (below), 124, 125, 127, 137, 139, 144, 147 (above), 147 (below), 156, 161, 164–167, 176, 179–181 (right), 182, 186/187

Bernhard Leitner and Elisabeth Kohlweiß (© Leitner): pp. 65, 72, 72a, 72b, 73, 74, 75, 79, 80, 80a, 80b, 85, 91–93, 97, 99, 101, 103, 113, 116, 120, 120a, 120b, 120 c, 131, 132, 134, 135, 150–152, 169, 170, 177 (above), 177 (below), 178, 181 (left)

Bernhard Leitner with Thomas Römer (© Leitner): p. 171

Moritz Nähr (1928): pp. 111, 163

Studio Hubert Urban (1972): pp. 62, 68, 69, 81, 84, 133, 153, 155, 173, 174

Landesbildstelle Wien (1959): p. 58

Bundesdenkmalamt Wien (1971): pp. 95, 183

Reproductions published with courtesy of

Wittgenstein Archive, Cambridge: pp. 7, 16, 27, 51, 53, 55–57, 86, 90, 98, 111, 163, 185

Johannes Koder: p. 157

Österreichische Nationalbibliothek: pp. 48a, 64, 83, 128, 154, 160, 184

Leitner Archive: pp. 8 (right), 59, 87, 89, 112

Drawings and Color Montages

Bernhard Leitner: pp. 31, 67, 70, 78, 82, 114, 119, 133, 134, 141–144, 146, 148, 149, 151, 152

I wish to thank Elisabeth Kohlweiß for her outstanding professional work and a highly valued collaboration. I am indebted to the University of Applied Arts in Vienna for supporting this project. Michael Nedo, director of the Wittgenstein Archive in Cambridge, with his profound knowledge of Wittgenstein's biography and philosophy has offered advice in many personal discussions. I am very grateful for his valuable contribution to this book. I also express my gratitude to the Bulgarian Cultural Institute in Vienna for permitting me to conduct the photographic and architectural survey of the Wittgenstein House.   B. L.